INTRODUCTION TO
NEW TESTAMENT EXEGESIS

Introduction to New Testament Exegesis

Werner Stenger

WILLIAM B. EERDMANS PUBLISHING COMPANY
GRAND RAPIDS, MICHIGAN

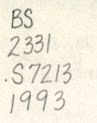
Translated and adapted from *Biblische Methodenlehre,*
published by Patmos Verlag, Düsseldorf
Copyright © 1987 Patmos Verlag Düsseldorf

First English translation copyright © 1993
by Wm. B. Eerdmans Publishing Co.
255 Jefferson Ave. S.E., Grand Rapids, Michigan 49503

Printed in the United States of America

Library of Congress Cataloging-in-Publication Data

Stenger, Werner, 1938-1990
[Biblische Methodenlehre. English]
Introduction to New Testament exegesis / Werner Stenger.
p.   cm.
Translation of: Biblische Methodenlehre.
Translated by Douglas W. Stott.
Includes bibliographical references and index.
ISBN 0-8028-0138-2 (paper)
1. Bible. N.T. — Hermeneutics. 2. Bible. N.T. — Criticism,
interpretation, etc. I. Title.
BS2331.S7213   1993
225.6'01—dc20   ˌ 93-26655
                                              CIP

In memory of
Heinrich Kahlefeld
(1903-1980)

Contents

Part Two: New Testament Exegesis in Practice

Contents

Foreword

by Bruce M. Metzger

Werner Stenger was born November 11, 1938, at Bad Kreuznach in Germany. After attending the modern language Gymnasium in Boppard (1952-57), he studied theology at the Catholic Theological Faculties of Trier, Innsbruck, and Munich, finally returning to Trier, where he received his diploma in 1963. After being consecrated as priest on June 28, 1963, in the Diocese of Trier, he devoted himself to work as a chaplain, giving religious instruction at four different kinds of schools: a high school, a technical school, a school for mentally handicapped students, and a vocational school. In addition he taught in a school for blind students.

Following a year of further study at the Institute for Catechetics and Homiletics in Munich (1966-67), Stenger became an assistant in Biblical Theology to Professor Franz Mussner at the newly established University of Regensburg. Here the development of the university library also brought him many additional responsibilities.

From 1973 to 1977 Stenger was docent for New Testament studies at the Institute for Catechetics and Homiletics as successor to Dr. Heinrich Kahlefeld, to whom the present book is dedicated. For much of the same period (1974-77) he also continued his duties as assistant to Professor Mussner at Regensburg. In April of 1977 Stenger became Professor of Biblical Theology at the Pedagogical High School of the Rheinland in Cologne. Three years later he was appointed Professor in the Faculty of Education at the University of Cologne, where he became the director of the Seminar for Theology and its Pedagogy.

Over the years Stenger gave sustained attention to various aspects of exegetical and theological study of Scripture. Besides writing half a dozen books, he published more than forty articles in journals and Festschriften and more than fifty exegetical or homiletical contributions in volumes intended for priests and catechists. All who knew him were saddened that the ravages of cancer cut short his life on June 7, 1990.

It is clear from this brief account that Professor Stenger gave attention not only to the subject matter and method of New Testament exegesis but also to the question of how best to teach that material to others. The title of this handbook thus identifies it as an "Introduction," suitable for those just beginning their study of New Testament exegesis.

Martin Luther more than once observed that unless people know what is being talked about, they cannot make sense of what is being said. In the first five chapters of this book Stenger carefully guides the reader from a consideration of "The Hermeneutical Foundation," which involves "The Art of Reading Well," to the "Fundamentals of New Testament Exegesis." The ten chapters that follow illustrate the methodology involved in an analysis of selected passages of the Gospels and the Epistles. As indicated in the Preface, the translator and the editor of the volume have adapted the bibliographical material to the needs of readers who are acquainted only with English. The following pages will thus be useful even to those whose background in the humanities has been minimal.

Princeton Theological Seminary, 1993

Preface

Werner Stenger's *Biblische Methodenlehre* has served many students working in the German language as a well-tuned and clear description and demonstration of the fundamental methods of biblical exegesis. In this translation and adaptation of his book a deliberate effort has been made to bring it fully into the world of English-speaking students and to fit it to the textbook needs of teachers in that world.

The most obvious change is that this English version of the book deals only with New Testament exegesis. This change was made because courses in exegesis in the English-speaking world normally deal only with the Hebrew Bible or the New Testament, not both together, and because, despite its title, *Biblische Methodenlehre* gave most of its attention to the New Testament. But though Prof. Stenger was known best as a New Testament scholar, his grasp of the influence of the Hebrew Bible's forms of expression on the New Testament writings is one of the clear values of this book.

Two things needed by a person being introduced to the methods of New Testament exegesis are knowledge of the standard tools and their use and knowledge of where to turn for help with particular kinds of issues. Prof. Stenger's recognition of these bibliographic needs is embodied in his explanations of use of these tools in the main body of the book, in footnotes, and in his final bibliographic chapter. The reader of this translation of his book is not expected to know any language other than English. No Greek is used — as in the book's German predecessor — and all the bibliographic material has been adapted for the reader of English. The bibliographic chapter has been almost entirely rewritten for this edition to include only works in English, though its basic outline is derived from the corresponding chapter in the German edition.

A few other changes have been made for the sake of clarity, including some shifting of material and dividing of long chapters. Prof. Stenger's "Hermeneutische Vorbemerkungen" have become the first chapter. An adaptation for English readers of his brief chapter 2 on Bible translations has been attached to that first chapter as "A Note on Translations," since it seemed worthwhile to give such guidance to students working only in English before plunging into issues of text criticism. Chapters 3, 4, and 5 of the present edition represent one chapter in the German original. Chapters 8 and 9 were also originally joined, as were chapters 10 and 11. The demonstrations of exegesis of parallel passages in these chapters were divided to provide a clearer and more convenient format for both students and teachers.

We have made every effort to make the explanations of technical terms of biblical scholarship directly serve the needs of readers of English. Some of Prof. Stenger's explanations have been adapted, simplified, or elaborated. Explanatory sentences and glosses have been added at a few points. On some occasions, footnotes commenting on the main text have been moved into the main text. Repetition and complexity of expression have been reduced on a number of occasions, though always without eliminating any of the substance of Prof. Stenger's discussion.

Transferring exegetical terminology from German to English is not a straightforward process, and terms distinguishing different approaches to biblical criticism do not always match up in the two languages. Our solution has been to favor the normal usage of New Testament scholars in the English-speaking world and to add explanatory footnotes where this involved significant departures from Prof. Stenger's distinctions and explanations, particularly in chapter 5. But the different focus that Prof. Stenger gives to "form criticism" in comparison with the traditional use of that term has been kept, though with slightly more deliberate attention to this shift in the term's meaning.

Our hope is that our efforts may enable Prof. Stenger's examples of patient explanation and thorough and critical exegesis to find a grateful audience in the English-speaking world.

Douglas W. Stott (translator)
John W. Simpson, Jr. (editor)

CHAPTER 1

The Hermeneutical Foundation

THE ART OF READING WELL

Despite this book's title, can we really speak of "*New Testament* exegesis"?
No, not if by that term we mean that the New Testament — or the whole
Bible for that matter — is to be read differently or interpreted by
methods different from those applied to the countless other books that
make up the enormous library of humankind. Serious biblical exegesis,
exegesis that reflects the intellectual gains of the modern age, stands or
falls with the principle of the equality of the exegetical methods applied
to the Bible with those applied to other books.

Johann Jakob Wettstein (1693-1754), whom we will meet again as
one of the founders of modern text criticism, stated this principle in an
addendum to his edition of the Greek New Testament: "Just as we read
the Holy Scriptures and secular laws — and all books, old and new —
with the same eyes, so also should we employ the same principles for
understanding the Scriptures that we use in understanding other
books."[1] It is the content of the Bible, not exegetical method itself, that
makes exegesis a theological discipline. Even if, as a person of faith, the
theologian ascribes greater authority to the Bible than to other books,
this decision of faith should not prompt the theologian to employ
methods in interpretation of the Bible fundamentally different from
those applied to any other written documents from the past or present.

1. J. J. Wettstein, "Über die Auslegung des Neuen Testaments," *Novum Testamentum Graecum* (Amsterdam, 1751/52) II, 875.

1

But, as Friedrich Nietzsche noted, theologians do indeed run the risk of exercising special privileges in their exposition of the Bible:

> Another sign of the theologian is his *incapacity for philology*. What is here meant by philology is, in a very broad sense, the art of reading well — of reading facts without falsifying them by interpretation, without losing caution, patience, delicacy, in the desire to understand. Philology as *ephexis* [i.e., persistence] in interpretation — whether it is a matter of books, the news in a paper, destinies, or weather conditions, not to speak of the "salvation of the soul.". . . The manner in which a theologian, in Berlin as in Rome, interprets a "verse of Scripture" or an event . . . is always so audacious that a philologist can only tear his hair.[2]

Nietzsche's remarks justifiably question the legitimacy of any theological "special hermeneutics" and lead ultimately to the all too often justified assertion that theologians belong to that group of poor readers who find in texts only what they already know. What echoes back to them from Scripture is the very words that they themselves have shouted into its forest. Any theologian seeking to avoid finding only himself or herself in Scripture must become a "philologist" in Nietzsche's sense, exercising "caution, patience, and delicacy" in "the art of reading well."

One prerequisite for this is to transfer the biblical texts from their apparent familiarity into an unfamiliar context, one that enables the reader to hear the Bible itself speaking, not merely the echo of his or her own voice. It is only such distance between reader and text that makes it possible to exclude any projections of meaning prompted by one's own ideas and desires and to open one's ears to the often alien voice of the text itself.

The methods of exegesis are intended to create this distance. They set themselves between the reader and the text as a lens through which the text is viewed and thus facilitate both observation and description by preventing the reader from appropriating the text directly. This may be painful for the reader who comes to the Bible expecting it to speak directly. Such a reader of the Bible will view the methods of exegesis as

---

2. F. Nietzsche, "The Antichrist," *The Portable Nietzsche*, trans. W. Kaufmann (New York: Viking, 1954) §52.

a burdensome obstacle in the way of his or her goal, which is an immediate understanding of the word of God.

But the idea of a direct encounter between the biblical text and the reader is useless for any disciplined and responsible dealing with the text that can yield an understanding that can be shared with those involved in other disciplines. Only exegetical methods that create distance can preserve a text from being violated by an understanding that finds in it only the pet ideas of the reader — usually with no awareness of what is happening. This is why, as Nietzsche himself knew, such exegetical methods are "what is for the longest time opposed by habits and laziness."[3]

OBJECTIVES AND METHODS OF EXEGESIS

But we can, in a sense, speak specifically of *New Testament* exegesis: Since the New Testament writings are nearly two thousand years old and belong both linguistically and conceptually to a world radically different from our own, specialized knowledge and skills are needed for New Testament exegesis. It is the adaptation of the various subdisciplines of exegesis to the nature of the text at hand that allows us to refer to exegesis of the New Testament in particular.

The subdisciplines of exegesis fall into three basic groups: Some seek to describe a text's *linguistic form* and underlying structures. Others look into the circumstances surrounding a text's *origin* and seek to identify its initial addressees. Finally, other methods investigate the *reception* a text has had in the course of its history and has in the present. But this third group of methods — when the text in question is the New Testament — is the task of every theological discipline, including ethics. Therefore, we must understand the specific discipline of *New Testament* exegesis as obligated in particular to describe the text's linguistic form and investigate the circumstances of its origin. New Testament exegesis is thus directed primarily toward *philological* and *historical* goals, and within this dual focus is called *historical-critical* exegesis.

Historical-critical exegesis includes within itself methods that are

---

3. Ibid. §59; cf. N. T. Wright, *The New Testament and the People of God* (Minneapolis: Fortress, 1992) 7, on "pre-critical" exegesis.

sometimes absolutized and presented as apparent alternatives to historical-critical exegesis. We can, for instance, understand some structuralist methodologies, which draw from the disciplines of linguistics and semiotics, as aimed toward more precise explication, correction, and expansion of the philological aspect of historical-critical exegesis. So we can seek to integrate such methodologies, along with discourse analysis and rhetorical analysis, into "form criticism," thus broadening the meaning of that methodological designation beyond the narrow tasks that it has traditionally represented. Furthermore, the historical aspect of historical-critical exegesis can include sociological and psychological approaches: Though such approaches will increasingly affect our understanding of the exegetical task in years to come, they were already implied in the principle formulated by Wettstein for the "historical" exegesis of the books of the New Testament, which accompanies "philological" exegesis:

> Put yourself into the position of those to whom the apostles first gave these books. Transport yourself in spirit to the time and place where they were first read. As far as possible, strive to understand the apostles' practices, customs, habits, opinions, ideas, proverbs, imagery, and vernacular and the way in which they tried to persuade others or elicit belief in their own arguments.[4]

The historical-critical method doubtlessly possesses a more colorful palette of possibilities because of these methodological developments. Through them its results have gained more precision and can be corrected from a larger number of directions. One can even say that the true internal system of the historical-critical method emerges fully only with the addition of insights from linguistics and literary criticism and that this development results in fundamental corrective insights — not least into the way the method is employed. But none of this constitutes a shift of the fundamental paradigm. The basic paradigm of historical-critical exegesis is able to embrace as integral elements both the ongoing development of its current methods and newly emerging methods.

Biblical exegesis may well appear to the beginner as splintered into a confusing variety of distinct individual methods. This array is all the

---

4. Wettstein, loc. cit.

more confusing because, despite much discussion, there is still no consensus regarding the definitions of these methods and the distinctions among them. One is thus well advised to keep in mind the basic ordering of exegetical methods described above: Some methods describe a text's linguistic form ("philological" methods), and some investigate the circumstances in which the text came into being ("historical" methods). This can also be stated in terms of the distinction between synchronic and diachronic approaches. In accordance with this distinction, Part One of this book will offer definitions and terminology for the individual methodological stages of exegesis, thus organizing them within the larger system of methods so that their interdependence and their unique functions are made clear. Then Part Two will apply the individual methods to selected New Testament texts. In the discussion of each text, a "philological" section will focus on the text's linguistic form and will precede a "historical" section focused on the reconstruction of the circumstances surrounding the text's origin and its significance in its original context.

THE THEOLOGICAL PROBLEMS OF THE HISTORICAL-CRITICAL METHOD

In working through the examples in Part Two the reader will doubtlessly be more aware than in Part One of the distance created by the historical-critical method. The results achieved with the texts chosen as examples should demonstrate that the hard work of exegesis is not merely an idle game, but is, rather, the inevitably arduous path to understanding a world that is not merely a reflection of our own. The historical distance brought to our attention by these methods liberates the texts from arbitrary readings and allows them to speak with their own voices. But it can also sometimes prevent them from being relevant for us. Having become objects from the past, the books of the New Testament are now made to speak only to that past. They fall silent when confronted with modern questions.

In the early days of the historical-critical method scholars optimistically anticipated that the "philological" understanding of a text's linguistic form and the "historical" illumination of its origin would naturally and almost effortlessly be followed by the resolution of the "theological" question of what the text says today. In any case, this is how Johann Salomo Semler (1725-1791), one of the fathers of historical-critical exegesis, viewed it:

> In a word, the most important part of hermeneutical skill is to be thoroughly and precisely acquainted with the Bible's *use of language,* and to distinguish precisely and keep in mind the *historical circumstances* of a biblical text. *One who has done so is then in a position to speak of these things in such a way that takes into account our own different time and circumstances.*[5]

This early optimism did not anticipate the theological problems that have arisen. These problems do not arise directly from the method. Historical-critical exegesis is aimed at setting the text at a distance from the reader in order to ensure authenticity to the reader's interpretation. The text has in this way become a partner allowed to speak with its own voice: The historical-critical reader no longer prescribes what it should say. But the unintended but inevitable result is that the words of the New Testament have come to be focused so intently on the historical situation of its origin that in many cases the possibility that it might be in dialogue with the present-day reader simply disappears.

Albert Schweitzer (1875-1965) described this dilemma in classic fashion:

> The study of the Life of Jesus has had a curious history. It set out in quest of the historical Jesus, believing that when it had found Him it could bring Him straight into our time as a Teacher and Saviour. It loosed the bands by which He had been riveted for centuries to the stony rocks of ecclesiastical doctrine, and rejoiced to see life and movement coming into the figure once more, and the historical Jesus advancing, as it seemed, to meet it. But He does not stay; He passes by our time and returns to His own. . . . by the same inevitable necessity by which the liberated pendulum returns to its original position.[6]

---

5. J. S. Semler, *Vorbereitung zur theologischen Hermeneutik, zur weiteren Beförderung des Fleißes angehender Gottesgelehrter nebst Antwort auf die Tübingische Vertheidigung der Apocalypsis* (Halle, 1760) 162.

6. A. Schweitzer, *The Quest of the Historical Jesus,* trans. W. Montgomery (New York: Macmillan, 1955) 399.

It goes beyond our tasks here to solve the problem of how one is to make that qualitative transition from the historical elements of biblical texts to theological statements that are relevant for today. Exegesis, like all the theological disciplines, continually breaks its teeth on this hard nut — to the extent that it is pursued honestly.[7] This introduction of the methods of New Testament exegesis will have done its job when, in addition to the presentation and application of exegetical methods, it also draws attention to the boundaries of historical-critical thinking, boundaries beyond which the real business of theological reflection begins.

But no one engaging in such reflection should attempt to skip over the preliminary task of historical-critical exegesis. To do so is to have one's theological statements leave the real world behind to ascend into an unreal realm.

A NOTE ON TRANSLATIONS

Translations of the New Testament into English are themselves a form of interpretation. They are not straightforward reproductions of the original text, but are, rather, witnesses to particular understandings of the text. They thus stand at the end of the interpretative process.

But for the person who is not able to read Greek, translations are necessarily the point of departure for work with the text. So such a reader of the New Testament is dependent on the work of others and has few ways of checking that work, the main method being that of comparing different translations. It is essential, therefore, that we be familiar with what takes place in translation.

The verb *translate* is derived from a Latin compound meaning "carry over" or "transfer." One who translates a text or statement from one language to another carries it, we might say, from one place to another. But while freight can be unaltered by shipment, a text translated from its original language into a target language invariably undergoes alterations of many kinds. The simple core meaning might be translatable, but it is

7. See, e.g., B. S. Childs, *Biblical Theology in Crisis* (Philadelphia: Westminster, 1970); P. Stuhlmacher, *Historical Criticism and Theological Interpretation of Scripture*, trans. R. A. Harrisville (Philadelphia: Fortress, 1977), esp. 61ff.; E. Krentz, *The Historical-Critical Method* (Philadelphia: Fortress, 1975) 73ff.; Wright, *The New Testament and the People of God* 8, 12f., 18-25.

impossible to transfer fully the phonological and grammatical elements of the original language. One can at best hope for an approximation, and even then it can be questionable whether the intended result of a text or statement remains the same in the target language.

An attempt to translate an Italian proverb, "*traduttore traditore,*" can illustrate the inevitability of alteration. The proverb plays on the phonological similarity of its two words. We confirm the accuracy of the proverb when we translate it into English: "The translator is a traitor": This *semantically* correct rendering is purchased at the price of alteration on the *phonological* and *grammatical* levels of language. English insists on filling out the proverb as a full sentence with definite and indefinite articles and a verb. It thus loses the connotation of inevitability that the original proverb conveys to the reader or hearer through the immediate succession of two nouns. Less is lost on the phonological level because we are also able to use two phonologically similar nouns, but even there the impact of the two nouns with no other words is lost. So the English translation, even if it represents the core meaning of the original proverb, has lost much in terms of its grammar, phonology, and consequent impact.

The alterations occurring in translation usually constitute a diminution of a text on various levels of language. Only rarely is something gained, and even then the proverb remains valid, since then, too, the translation would ultimately not be an "accurate" rendering of the original.

So a translation must always work against either its original language or its target language. In the translator's efforts to offer a substitute for the original, he or she must choose between two fundamental possibilities, both of which accomplish less than the ideal goal of total semantic, grammatical, and phonological equivalence. One of these possibilities, which translation theorists call *"formal equivalence,"* is oriented toward the linguistic *form* of the original and seeks to imitate that form in word order, syntax, and, if possible, in phonology. The other possibility, that of *"dynamic equivalence"* or *"functional equivalence,"* seeks to recreate by means available in the target language the impact or effect a text has among its hearers or readers in the original language. An essential prerequisite for evaluating any translation is the step of determining where it fits on the scale from "formal equivalence" to "dynamic equivalence."[8]

---

8. For further discussion of this distinction see E. A. Nida, *Toward a Science of Translating* (Leiden: Brill, 1964) 156-92, or, more briefly, B. M. Metzger, "Theories of the Translation Process," *Bibliotheca Sacra* 150 (1993) 140-50.

The Good News Bible is explicitly identified with the goal of dynamic equivalence. The translator's task was to discern the meaning of the original and then "to express that meaning in a manner and form easily understood by the readers. . . . [T]here has been no attempt to reproduce in English the parts of speech, sentence structure, word order, and grammatical devices of the original languages."[9] At the other end of the scale we might mention "interlinear" New Testaments, though they are not intended to function alone as translations.[10]

The classic example of a formal equivalence translation is the American Standard Version of 1901 and the closely related English Revised Version. But the predecessor of these translations, the King James Version, is itself to a large extent a formal equivalence translation. Among more recent versions in the King James-American Standard tradition, the New American Standard Bible is more of a formal equivalence translation than the Revised Standard Version, whose successor, the New Revised Standard Version, is a bit closer to a dynamic equivalence translation than its immediate predecessor. Other commonly used translations, such as the New International Version, the Jerusalem Bible and New Jerusalem Bible, and the Revised English Bible and its predecessor, the New English Bible, are generally closer to dynamic equivalence translations than the successors of the King James Version.

All these translations fluctuate to some degree between the two intentions of doing justice to the original text in the sense of formal equivalence and of presenting the reader or hearer with a functional equivalent. Among the criteria deserving attention when evaluating a translation, intended use is certainly the most decisive: There are great differences among use of the Bible in, for example, private devotional reading, liturgy, and the university classroom. Here, in an introduction to New Testament exegetical methods for those who may not be acquainted with Greek, we are best served by translations approximating formal equivalence. Therefore, we often quote the Revised Standard Version (RSV), though sometimes a translation, also tending toward formal equivalence, is formulated for the specific need as it arises.

9. *The Good News Bible: The Bible in Today's English Version* (New York: American Bible Society, 1978), preface.

10. See, e.g., the interlinear translation by A. Marshall and its introduction (pp. vi-xvi) in *The NRSV-NIV Parallel New Testament in Greek and English* (Grand Rapids: Zondervan, 1990).

PART ONE

FUNDAMENTALS OF NEW TESTAMENT EXEGESIS

CHAPTER 2

The Problem of the Original Text

When we read the Greek New Testament, it is not the original text that is read, but the results of a scholarly attempt to rediscover as closely as possible the original text. We have only handwritten copies of the New Testament documents as they came from the hands of the New Testament authors — and copies of copies.

In antiquity such copies were made by slaves or paid professional scribes, and in the Middle Ages they were made by monks. It was an arduous task, and this we know from what scribes occasionally wrote in the margins of manuscripts: "Writing bows one's back, thrusts the ribs into one's stomach, and fosters a general debility of the body," laments one of the copyists. Another breathes a sigh of relief: "As travellers rejoice to see their home country, so also is the end of a book to those who toil [in writing]."[1]

Despite and even because of the efforts of these scribes, errors crept into the text during the copying procedure. To err is human, though matters get even worse when the copyist reflects on and then consciously alters something in the text. The copies were checked by specialized editors, but the manuscript tradition of the New Testament

---

1. These examples come from a very readable book on text criticism by B. M. Metzger, *The Text of the New Testament* (New York/London: Oxford University Press, 1964; 3rd ed., 1992) 17f. Two other important books are K. Aland and B. Aland, *The Text of the New Testament: An Introduction to the Critical Editions and to the Theory and Practice of Modern Textual Criticism,* trans. E. Rhodes (Grand Rapids, Eerdmans: [2]1989), and E. J. Epp and G. D. Fee, *Studies in the Theory and Method of New Testament Textual Criticism* (Grand Rapids: Eerdmans, 1993).

has some 250,000 instances in which manuscripts deviate from one another. We refer to these deviations as textual variants or readings. *Text criticism seeks to clarify just which of these textual variants stood in the original text.*

As those who apply a rigorous scholarly method, text critics are not permitted to make arbitrary decisions. They must present reasons and criteria for each decision regarding the text. Only with such supporting arguments can they assert that the reading of one manuscript is more true to the original text at a given point than is another manuscript. Such criteria include the *number* of witnesses, the *age* of a given manuscript, and the *geographical distribution* of a particular reading. As a rule, the older a variant is, the more manuscripts attesting it, and the greater its geographical distribution, the more likely it is to be original. If, for example, we find a certain reading attested in manuscripts from Egypt, North Africa, Asia Minor, and Gaul, it generally takes precedence over the variant attested by only a single manuscript from, say, Gaul.

But text criticism does not just mechanically enumerate the age and number of manuscripts and the geographical distribution of readings. In addition to these *external* factors, other questions come into play that deal with the *interior* elements of the text, that is, with its meaning.

SMALL LETTERS, PROFOUND EFFECT

We can show this with three examples.

Apostolic Decree or Abbreviated Decalogue? (Acts 15:29)

Acts 15 reports on what has come to be called the Apostolic Council. This meeting of church leaders dealt with whether Gentiles should be circumcised in the Jewish fashion on entering the church. This question was hotly debated at the time, and came to have far-reaching implications for the future of Christianity as a world religion separate from Judaism. The result of the council according to Acts was the regulations of James, or what is called the Apostolic Decree. James, Jesus' brother, advised the council not to require circumcision of Gentiles. Gentiles should, however, according to one reading, "abstain from what has been sacrificed to idols, from blood, from what has been strangled, and from unchastity" (v. 29).

These four prohibitions encourage Gentile Christians to be considerate of Jewish Christians, that is, to refrain in community life from certain acts that would have seemed disgusting or impious to Jews because of their religious training and cultural background. Such acts included eating meat that had been sacrificed to idols or that had not been ritually butchered (and so had "blood" in it or had been "strangled") and marriage to closer relatives than was permitted among Jews ("unchastity"). These regulations sought to prevent any offense to Jews and so alleviate problems that might arise in eucharistic table fellowship in Christian communities composed of both Jews and Gentiles.

But a manuscript (known as Codex D) that originated in the Romanized West during the sixth century offers us a different version of James's regulations. Here he requires that Gentile Christians "abstain from what has been sacrificed to idols, from blood, and from unchastity — and not do to others what they do not wish to be done to themselves." This reading says both more and less than the reading we have already looked at. It omits "what is strangled" and adds a negative version of the "Golden Rule" (cf. the positive formulation in Matt 7:12).

The text critic is faced with the question of which reading is closer to the original. External criteria used to answer this question include that the *majority* of manuscripts, including many *older* manuscripts, attest the first of these two readings and that the second reading is attested only by the relatively *late* Codex D. Codex D comes from the sixth century, while the oldest papyri we possess are from the second century. Furthermore, Codex D was circulated only among churches in the West, while the first reading has far greater *geographical distribution.*

The text critic can refer not only to these *external* criteria, but also to *internal* criteria, since the differences between the two readings affect the meaning of the passage. A copyist has consciously altered the sense of the text: The Golden Rule shows that the second reading is no longer concerned merely with regulations affecting the relations of Jews and Gentiles in Christian communities, but now with moral demands. In the light of this addition, "what has been sacrificed to idols" no longer prohibits eating meat from pagan sacrificial offerings, but is rather a prohibition of pagan worship. "Unchastity" is no longer directed to

15

keeping Gentiles from entering into marriages with relatives too close for Jewish custom, but is rather directed against sexual immorality in general. "Blood" is now a prohibition of murder. Since the reference to "what is strangled" was not compatible with this new understanding of the Apostolic Decree, the copyist simply omitted it. The copyist thus was able to emphasize with the decree the most important of the Ten Commandments: those prohibiting idolatry, adultery, and murder.

The text critic will conclude by pointing out that as far as the *history of the text* is concerned, this later version reflects the historical situation of a church that has already outgrown the problems arising between Christian Jews and Christian Gentiles. This missionary church of a time far removed from that of the New Testament was set in the midst of a pagan environment and sought to present the Christian ethos in terms of the Decalogue and the Golden Rule.

The evidence thus points the text critic toward identifying the first reading that we have examined as closer to the original. This decision is reflected in modern editions of the Greek New Testament and modern translations of Acts.[2]

Jesus' Physical Father or Mary's Betrothed? (Matt 1:16)

What is probably the original text of Matt 1:16 reads: "Jacob begat Joseph, the husband of Mary, *of whom Jesus was born*, he who is called 'Christ.'" But an Old Syriac translation offers the following variant: "Jacob begat Joseph. Joseph, who was betrothed to Mary, the virgin, *begat Jesus*, he who is called 'Christ.'"

From a text-critical perspective there is hardly any problem here. The first reading certainly deserves precedence over the second on the basis of the age, quality, number, and geographical distribution of the supporting manuscripts. The second reading is attested by only one — albeit relatively old — manuscript, and that manuscript itself is a Syriac translation.

2. E.g., the standard editions of the Greek text: *The Greek New Testament,* ed. K. Aland, M. Black, C. M. Martini, B. M. Metzger, and A. Wikgren (third ed., corrected; New York: United Bible Societies, 1983) 477f.; *Novum Testamentum Graece* (Nestle-Aland), from the same editors (Stuttgart: Deutsche Bibelstiftung, [26]1979) 367. See also the discussion in B. M. Metzger, *A Textual Commentary on the Greek New Testament* (New York: United Bible Societies, 1971) 429-34.

In addition to these *external* factors, *internal* factors also suggest that the first reading is closer to the original. It describes Joseph as Mary's "husband." The second reading presents Mary as "betrothed" to Joseph, and this we may view as an assimilation on the part of the copyist to the context, since v. 18 reads: "When [Jesus'] mother Mary had been betrothed to Joseph." Furthermore, the description of Mary as a "virgin" is another assimilation, since it apparently anticipates what is said in v. 23: "Behold, the *virgin* will conceive. . . ."

This Syriac variant presents *Joseph as Jesus' physical father* ("Joseph begat Jesus"), and the text critic can understand this in one of two ways. On the one hand it may be

> a purely mechanical imitation of the preceding pattern in the genealogy. Since every name in the genealogy up to Joseph is written twice in succession, it may be that the scribe of the Sinaitic Syriac (or an ancestor of this manuscript) carelessly followed the stereotyped pattern and in ver. 16, having made the initial mistake of repeating the word "Joseph," went on to produce [this] reading. . . .[3]

But this reading can also be explained by consideration of *text history,* that is, of the changing circumstances that affected the production of the various manuscripts. The reason that the passive formulation "of whom Jesus was born" was replaced by the presentation of Joseph as Jesus' physical father can be found in doctrinal developments that are external to the text itself. Certain Christian circles articulated their faith in Jesus as the Christ without using the theological idea of the "virgin birth." The later confessional position of the church identified these circles as "heretical." That a relatively early (fourth-century) Old Syriac translation expunges the idea of the "virgin birth" suggests that this translation originated in Nestorian circles, probably when the topic of the "virgin birth" had already been made a criterion for orthodoxy by the church. For only when this topic had become problematic could it have become necessary for some Christians to alter the New Testament text in order to suggest that their rejection of belief in the "virgin birth" was biblically supported.[4]

---

3. Metzger, *Textual Commentary* 7.
4. See the more detailed discussion in Metzger, *Textual Commentary* 2-7.

Intentional or Accidental? (1 Tim 3:16)

The short christological hymn in 1 Tim 3:16 was probably not composed by the author of the pseudonymous first letter of Paul to Timothy, but is rather quoted by the author, as can be seen from the citation formula that introduces the hymn and places it within its textual environment (see p. 123 below): "Great indeed, as is known, is the mystery of our religion. . . ." The hymn then follows:

> He who was manifested in the flesh,
>> was justified in the Spirit,
>> was seen by angels,
>> was preached among the nations,
>> was believed on in the world,
>> was taken up into glory.

This hymn — quite a work of art in the Greek original — speaks of Jesus' incarnation and exaltation in the first and second lines, the heavenly and earthly proclamation of Jesus in the third and fourth, and the earthly and heavenly acceptance of this proclamation in the fifth and sixth. The only problem arising in the textual tradition of this hymn is the first word. Manuscripts attest three different readings:

1. "*He who* [Greek OC] was manifested in the flesh,"
2. "*God* [abbreviated in Greek as $\overline{\Theta C}$] was manifested in the flesh," and
3. "*That which* [O] was manifested in the flesh."

External factors — the number of witnesses and their geographical distribution — clearly support the originality of the first reading. *Internal* considerations also prompt us to give priority to this reading. The third reading is clearly recognizable as an assimilation of the copyist to the preceding citation formula, since the neuter relative pronoun, translated as "that which," would then go with the neuter "mystery of our religion." But the first reading, with the masculine pronoun translated as "He who," yields a certain grammatical abruptness when the hymn is appended to the citation formula.

And it is easiest to explain the second reading as the result of a copyist's error, given the similarity in appearance of "God" and "He who" as they would have been written in Greek. A deliberate alteration is also conceivable, since the pronoun "who" without an antecedent actually leaves unresolved just who it was that was "manifested in the flesh." So "*God* was manifested in the flesh" can be explained as a copyist's attempt to clarify an ambiguity. However, then, we understand its origin, the second reading is much less likely than the first to be original.

Text history is what we are doing when we try to clarify when and how individual manuscripts and readings originated. 1 Tim 3:16 is a paradigmatic example of text history, and it shows how serious the interpretation of a single letter could be.

The reading "*He who* was manifested in the flesh" had beome established in the Byzantine church by the sixth century. A church history of the time tells of "Macedonius, Bishop of Constantinople [495-511]," who was "excommunicated by Emperor Anastasius because he falsified the gospel, specifically the apostle's statement 'who was manifested in the flesh, justified in the Spirit.'" He altered one letter in 1 Tim 3:16 — adding a line to change O to Θ — with the intention of having "God" (ΘC) be merely "manifested" in the "flesh," that is, not *become* flesh. But this same understanding had been what had prompted the charge of heresy against the monk Nestorius, who had reportedly asserted that the incarnation was merely a kind of indwelling of God-Logos in the man Jesus, so that there was never any real unity of essence. That Macedonius read "God was manifested in the flesh" in his Bible was reason enough to associate him with that "heretic," though in reality there was no reason to doubt Macedonius's orthodoxy. His excommunication and murder at the behest of the emperor were actually politically motivated. Today the Greek Orthodox Church venerates him as a saint.

About a thousand years later the reading "God was manifested in the flesh" had become established in the western church, specifically in what later became known as the "Textus Receptus." The irony of history was that Johann Jakob Wettstein (1693-1754), one of the fathers of modern text criticism, who at that time was a pastor in Basel and taught at the university there, challenged this reading by referring to the text of the Codex Alexandrinus. He believed the original reading was "*He who* was manifested in the flesh." What had counted as orthodoxy in Macedonius's time was reason enough to accuse Wettstein of expunging Christ's divinity from Scripture. Branded as a heretic,

Wettstein had to leave the university and city of Basel and move to Holland.[5]

Not only, as the proverb goes, do books have their own destinies: Mere letters of the alphabet can prompt a turn of events that becomes a threat to those involved. And this is not something that occurs only in the past.

TEXT CRITICISM IN PRACTICE

These three examples have given us a very basic look at the presuppositions and procedures of text criticism. They have shown that the text critic must bring far more skills to his or her craft than just a precise acquaintance with the language of the New Testament. In theory, text criticism is part of exegesis, since its job is to provide the prerequisite for exegesis, that is, the text itself. But in practice, text criticism has become an independent discipline. The typical exegetical scholar of today is usually capable of following text-critical discussions well enough to reach his or her own conclusions with regard to the original text. But only rarely is the exegetical scholar also enough of a specialist in text criticism to undertake text-critical research from the ground up, that is, beginning with the original Greek manuscripts themselves.

Any exegete, however, has access to the results of text-critical scholarship in the critical editions of the New Testament.[6] These editions represent the results of text-critical evaluations of the various manuscripts, and for that reason include a "critical apparatus" printed below the actual reconstructed text. This apparatus notes important variants from the manuscripts and identifies those manuscripts with a special set of abbreviations. This apparatus allows the exegete to know the reasons that the text critic has chosen the particular version of a given passage offered in the reconstructed text. And it also offers information on other variants that might prompt the exegete to make a different decision regarding the original text.

5. More of this history is told in W. Stenger, "Textkritik als Schicksal," *Biblische Zeitschrift* 19 (1975) 240-47; idem, "Kleine Buchstaben, große Wirkung. Beschreibung der Fälle X und Y nebst Nachspiel als Parabel zum Fall K," *Imprimatur* 13 (1980) 8-11.
6. See n. 2 above.

Such occasional disagreements find expression in scholarly commentaries.[7] Everyone using these commentaries should have at least a passing acquaintance with the methods of text criticism, in order simply to be able to follow the discussion.

The fundamental message of this very basic introduction to text criticism is that even at the level of simple textual tradition or transmission we are already dealing with *interpretation.* We do not have direct access to the meaning of a biblical text and its theological assertions — or even to the text itself. By the very nature of the material our only access is by exegetical methods.

---

7. See, e.g., the discussions of the text of the Apostolic Decree in H. Conzelmann, *Acts of the Apostles* (Philadelphia: Fortress, 1987) 118; F. F. Bruce, *The Acts of the Apostles: Greek Text with Introduction and Commentary* (Grand Rapids: Eerdmans, [3]1990) 342f.

CHAPTER 3

Exegetical Methods I:
First Considerations

What Is a "Text"?

Biblical exegesis has its own specialized terminology, which, in part, it shares with other disciplines that deal with language and literature.[1] Specialized terminology is necessary in every field of scholarship because it lends precision to concepts and allows for more economical communication. In this book you will see some basic definitions and distinctions of terms, though the discussion will not go too deeply into the thicket of scholarly jargon.

When we use the word "text" to designate the object examined by exegesis, you are right to guess that this refers to something written. But this understanding does not go far enough. Just what is a "text?" Specialists are far from agreement in their use of the term.[2] I have no choice but to cut a path through the jungle of usage by providing a clear definition, knowing full well that what I consider pedagogically cleared

---

1. Text criticism, e.g., is also exercised in relation to literatures other than the Bible. The discussion of translations at the end of chapter 1 used several terms from the specialized vocabulary of linguistics.

2. "Linguistics offers various definitions of a 'text' depending on whether the orientation is toward ontology, toward function and intention, toward the immanence of the text, toward analysis of communication, or theoretically toward the act of speaking itself" (P. G. Müller, "Text," *Lexikon exegetischer Fachbegriffe* [Stuttgart and Kevelaer, 1985] 242). See also A. C. Thiselton, *New Horizons in Hermeneutics: The Theory and Practice of Transforming Biblical Reading* (Grand Rapids: Zondervan, 1992) 15, 19f., 49, 55-75.

land may be perceived by others as scholarly deforestation. By the term "text" I mean *a cohesive and structured expression of language that, while at least relatively self-contained, intends a specific effect.*

The first line of the return address I write on envelopes is:

from: Werner Stenger

Let us examine whether, according to the definition I have given, this short set of words is a "text."

"Cohesive and Structured"

As a first stage of investigation, I note that there are three words in the example and I note also other formal elements, that two of the words begin with capital letters and that there is a mark of punctuation indicating that the break between "from:" and "Werner Stenger" is thus emphasized more strongly than that between "Werner" and "Stenger." In other words, there is a stronger *divider between the first two words than between the second and the third. I do not make arbitrary divisions: My analysis of the text into segments* makes use of specific criteria, that is, structural signals, that enable me to recognize something of the nature of the relationships between the various parts.

This analysis is then confirmed at the level of meaning, that is, at the semantic level. Viewed semantically, the word "Werner" goes with the word "Stenger" and vice versa: The first name "Werner" specifies a smaller group among those who have the family name "Stenger," and "Stenger" conversely specifies a smaller group among those who have the first name "Werner." Each of the two segments defines the other more precisely by limiting its meaning. The segments work together, that is, they exhibit *coherence* and are organized in a semantic *structure.* The word "from:" indicates that the two subsequent words form the name of the person who has written the letter; it is, therefore, the segment to which the other two segments are subordinated. So the semantic structure is one of hierarchical relationships. It is only by means of this structure that this set of words constitutes a unified whole with a self-contained overall meaning.

"At Least Relatively Self-Contained and Intending a Specific Effect"

A person does not use language merely to create words, but also, whether speaking or writing, in order to reach a specific and intentional goal in relation to the hearer or reader. When I write my return address on envelopes, I hope that those I write to understand the meaning of this text (its semantic level), that is, that it is I who have written to them. But I also intend to attain a further goal in relation to them: I hope that they write back to me. Only when *meaning* and *function,* that is, the text in its semantic and pragmatic dimensions, are grasped together can one determine whether the set of words in question is "relatively self-contained." Our example text is "self-contained," but only as it is *imbedded* in a larger text, my street address.

As a result of being imbedded in a larger whole, "from: Werner Stenger" can be regarded as only a "partial text." But even so its function by itself, that of letting the recipient know from whom he is receiving the letter so that he or she can perhaps write back, prevents it from being, strictly speaking, a "textual component." "From:" taken by itself is a textual component or constituent part of our text, as are "Werner" and "Stenger" taken by themselves or together. These *textual components* or *segments* have no function of their own within the framework of the text, but rather work together with each other to constitute the whole of the *text* from a syntactic and semantic perspective.

Summary

To this point I have undertaken three methodologically distinct procedures:

1. I have *analyzed* a given text into its constituent parts.
2. I have *reassembled* those parts to see how they function in sequence as *coherent* parts of a specific *structure* at the level of syntax and semantics.

I have therefore begun with analysis and synthesis. And finally, at the level of pragmatic impact,

3. I have *determined* the text's *intention.*

This process can be represented graphically in this way:

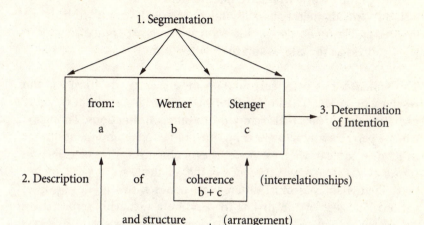

Synchrony and Diachrony

Let us conduct a small experiment with our example text by imagining it written on the envelope where the addressee's name usually is.

This new situation of the text does not affect the segmentation. "From:" is still the textual component to which the other two components are subordinated. Syntactically and semantically the coherence between "Werner" and "Stenger" also remain as described above.

But the meaning of "from:" is obscured, since it no longer fits the changed situation and intention of the text, which now indicates who the letter is written to, not who wrote it. A purely descriptive understanding of these textual components in their coherence and structure, as we did above — simply describing what is there — leads us into a dead end. At best we can conclude that we are dealing with a meaningless or incomprehensible text.

And yet the post office apparently did understand the meaning and intention of this very text. A while back I received a letter from some friends in France, and the addressee was "from: Werner Stenger." One need not be Sherlock Holmes or an ingenious postal expert to reconstruct how this unusual address came about:

1. I wrote a letter to my French friends with the return address beginning with "from: Werner Stenger."
2. My friends then apparently misunderstood "from:" to be something like an academic title and used an exact copy of my return address as the address on their letter to me.[3]

The semantic obscurity surrounding the meaning of "from:" is thus resolved by an explanation of the historical origin of the text, an explanation that breaks that history down into two situations. Though we cannot perceive any new meaning for the textual component "from:" in its new context, we have nonetheless come up with a plausible *historical explanation* for its presence in that context.

Textual analysis must differentiate between two modes of observation. The goal of the first is to describe a text with respect to its coherence, structure, and function, that is, with respect to its extant form. The second attempts to comprehend and explain that form as the result of a historical process. Drawing on terminology going back to the Swiss linguist Ferdinand de Saussure (1857-1913), one can use the term *synchronic* for the first mode of observation, that which is aimed at describing the present condition of the text, that is, *what it is*. One can then use the term *diachronic* for historical-genetic explanation of the text, that is, for explanation of *how it came to be what it is*.

The point of departure for diachronic explanation is always something that cannot be explained synchronically. The sequence of synchronic and diachronic modes of observation is not arbitrary: *Before* the question of *how the text has come to be* (diachronic study) stands the question of *what it is* at a given point in time (synchronic study). The exegete must distinguish, as we did in our example, between *descriptive-synchronic* methods and *genetic-historical*, that is, *diachronic* methods. Synchronic procedures always precede diachronic procedures.[4] The latter come into play when synchronic description cannot sufficiently explain the present state of a text.

---

3. Prof. Stenger's French friends deserve the explanation that his return address began, in German, with "Abs.: Werner Stenger," "Abs.:" being an abbreviation for *Absender* [trans. and ed.].

4. It is no accident that Carl von Linné (1707-78) wrote *A General System of Nature* (1735) a century before Charles Darwin (1809-82) could undertake his presentation of *The Origin of Species* (1859), understanding the various animal species as results of an evolutionary process. Synchrony seems to precede diachrony in the natural sciences as well.

"Form criticism," as the term is used in this book, represents the synchronic procedures carried out by the exegete, that is, all considerations of the unique structure of a text. These procedures will be described in the next chapter. Diachronic exegetical methods will be described in chapter 5. They include tradition criticism, source criticism, and redaction criticism, which are based on the discernment of tensions within the text, and genre criticism.

CHAPTER 4

Exegetical Methods II:
The Form of the Text

THE TWO TASKS OF FORM CRITICISM

Form criticism is, then, synchronically oriented. Its goal is description of the shape and function of the one specific self-contained text. The text that form criticism is concerned with might be a whole Gospel or letter, or it might be a relatively self-contained part of a whole document (a miracle story in one of the Gospels, for instance). Such a partial text is imbedded in the larger text but possesses, nonetheless, its own discernible function. Here we will generally use the term "text" to refer to both whole documents and smaller texts.

Form criticism, as we will be using the term in this book, has two tasks. The first is segmentation of the text or partial text, that is, analysis of it according to certain criteria into its constituent elements or textual components. When we deal with partial texts this first stage must include delimitation of the partial text from the preceding and following material.

The second task of form criticism is description of the coherence and structure of the text or partial text. We determine how the elements that constitute the text, that is, the textual components, are interconnected syntactically and semantically within the text (coherence) and related within its overall arrangement (structure) in such a way that the meaning and intended effect (semantics, determination of intention) of the text are made possible.[1]

---

1. The *basis* for diachronic analysis, i.e., for the beginnings of source criticism, is already laid at this point, since breaks in coherence, i.e., disturbances in the text's

Form criticism proceeds, therefore, from analysis to synthesis.

PREPARING FOR SEGMENTATION OF THE TEXT

As was the case with the text used as an example in chapter 3, we need certain criteria to guide us in the segmentation of New Testament texts or partial texts. In the New Testament, chapter and verse numbers might seem to provide this kind of division, but they are unsuitable for that purpose, since they were added long after the composition of the New Testament documents and are often fairly arbitrary. They cannot relieve us of the task of organizing the text in such a way that its internal relationships and structures become clear.

A first step in this task can be to write out the text with line breaks, as if it were a poem. The breaks should be placed after each clause. A general rule is that each verb belongs to and thus identifies a separate clause. Breaks should also distinguish any units of language that fulfill self-contained functions within themselves, such as vocatives, interjections, or individual items in lists, except where there are groups of similar items within a list that should be kept together (e.g., the four or five groups in the list of "works of the flesh" in Gal 5:19-21). Subordinate infinitive constructions should not be placed on separate lines of their own, since they do not constitute the kind of relatively autonomous language unit that we are attempting to identify.

When you write the text out in lines according to these criteria, include the original verse numbers and label the successive lines in each verse as *a, b, c,* and so on. When a clause or language unit is interrupted by another unit imbedded in it and then taken up again, label the imbedded element with both a letter and a number (e.g., a^1). These steps are illustrated in the diagram of Luke 18:9-14 on p. 30.[2]

---

network of relationships, sometimes become visible here. But it is not appropriate to move ahead to that at this stage. Form criticism is concerned with giving the text the benefit of the doubt for as long as possible, assuming, i.e., that it is indeed coherent or consistent, that it is readable. Any fundamental mistrust is ill-advised, though it must not be replaced by an equally detrimental naive trust, since identifying tensions in the text has merely been delayed, and by no means suspended.

2. This example is from H. Schweizer, "Wovon reden die Exegeten? Zum Verständnis der Exegese als verstehender und deskriptiver Wissenschaft," *Theologische*

Luke 18:9-14

> 9a He told this parable to some trusting in themselves
> a₁ that they were righteous
> a and despising others:
> 10a "Two men went up to the temple to pray.
> b One was a Pharisee,
> c and the other was a tax collector.
> 11a The Pharisee stood praying with himself,
> b 'O God,
> c I thank you
> d that I am not like other people,
> e robbers,
> f unjust,
> g adulterers,
> h or even like this tax collector.
> 12a I fast twice a week,
> b I give tithes of all
> c that I receive.'
> 13a The tax collector, standing far away, would not even lift up
>   his eyes to heaven,
> b but hit against his chest, saying,
> c 'O God,
> d be merciful to me a sinner.'
> 14a I tell you,
> b this man went down to his house justified rather than the other."
> c For everyone exalting himself will be humbled,
> d but the one humbling himself will be exalted.

SEGMENTATION OF THE TEXT

Segmentation of a text cannot be undertaken arbitrarily. It must follow certain signs in the text, *text dividers,* that indicate that breaks of a higher

---

Quartalschrift 164 (1984) 3ff., though the suggestions made there for the original Greek cannot be transferred to English without giving, as here, a stilted translation. The problem is that Greek participles and infinitive constructions, which according to Schweizer should not be on separate lines, are normally rendered in English as independent and dependent clauses, which would suggest that they be placed on separate lines. But here, for the purpose of illustration, the translation follows Greek grammatical structure more closely.

level than line breaks should be made in some places and not in others. Because we are working with a translation, these text dividers or structural signals must be translinguistic, applicable, that is, both in the original Greek of the text and in English.

Without trying to exhaust the possibilities, let us look at some of these text dividers or structural signals.

Text Dividers in Narrative Texts

Such text dividers can be quite varied, depending on the kind of text we are dealing with, even though certain kinds of dividers occur in all types of texts. In *narrative texts,* including the example above, particular attention should be paid to indications of *time, place,* or *speaker, indications of which persons* are included in the action, and indications of progress in the *action.*

Indications of time and place are of special significance, since "in narrative texts the sphere of objects and events is characterized by its relation to space and time. . . . Temporal progression is most important; changes in place usually play a role only in connection with temporal progression." Such indications of time include those that mark off *episodes,* that is, groups of events that are unique in themselves, and those that indicate *repetitions* of a group of events. The first of these, indicators of episodes, include both those that speak of the point of departure for an episode and those that speak simply of succession.[3]

Indications of place can be differentiated similarly: A narrative can name places in which events occur (and can thus name more specific locations within preceding comprehensive indications of place), or a location can be named as the point of departure or goal of a given movement. If we look at the parable told by Jesus in Luke 18:10-13, we see that it has no signals at all of temporal organization: As a parable it possesses some amount of timeless validity. But it does use indications of place: The action begins with two men going to the temple in Jerusalem, and the shift of attention from one man to the

---

3. E. Gülich, "Ansätze zu einer kommunikationsorientierten Erzähltextanalyse (am Beispiel mündlicher und schriftlicher Erzähltexte)," *Zeitschrift für Literaturwissenschaft und Linguistik,* Beiheft 4: *Erzählforschung 1,* ed. W. Haubrichs (Göttingen, 1976) 242f.

other includes an indication of a more specific kind of location in the temple (v. 13).

Changes in which characters are, so to speak, on stage also function to structure narrative and are thus counted among text dividers or structural indicators. For example, a new person is introduced into the action, or a person who is otherwise part of the story does not participate in the action in a partial text, or the action in a partial text takes different persons as its point of departure.[4]

Other structural signals can be added to these. The beginning and end of Luke 18:9-14 are marked by *discourse introductions:* At the beginning the narrator introduces Jesus as the speaker, that is, as the narrator of a parable (v. 9a). That Jesus is not mentioned by name is one indication that this is not an independent or completely new textual beginning, in which case the narrator would have to introduce his participants. What we have is, instead, just the beginning of a partial text. Jesus himself as the narrator uses discourse introductions in the parable (vv. 11a, 13b) and then uses another discourse introduction (v. 14a) to move beyond the role of narrator.

Text Dividers in Poetry and Nonnarrative Prose

This concluding section of our example text (Luke 18:14) can itself be divided into three parts: First, Jesus uses a discourse introduction to emphasize the concluding part of his own discourse: "I tell you . . ." Then comes the narrative conclusion to the parable, which has thus been emphasized: "This man went down to his house justified rather than the other." And finally, the writer of the Gospel gives his commentary on the whole parable (though perhaps it is to be included with the preceding words of Jesus): "For everyone who exalts himself will be humbled, but the one who humbles himself will be exalted."

This concluding remark (v. 14cd), which is thus distinguished from the narrative functionally as commentary on the narrative, also acquires a certain independence as a self-enclosed textual segment by being structured in antithetical parallelism, its two parts (c and d) giving the two opposing sides of a single principle.

The poetry of our own literary tradition was — in the past far

4. Cf. ibid., 243.

more than now — normally characterized by parallelism of sounds at the ends of lines, that is, by rhyme. This was an identifying feature of poetry and with strophic division and meter was one of the significant structural signals in poetic texts.

But the poetry of the Hebrew Bible employs, rather than rhyme, syntactic and semantic parallelism, which is, in effect, a rhyming of concepts or imagery instead of sounds. In this kind of parallelism, the second of two successive lines expresses

- the same thing as the first line, but in different words (synonymous parallelism),
- the completion of what is expressed in the first line (synthetic parallelism), or
- a contrast to what is expressed in the first line (antithetical parallelism).

Poetic language is used in these ways to set concepts and imagery in order and thus to give structure to poetic texts.

The parallelism of Hebrew poetry has influenced the manner of expression in many places in the New Testament.[5] Synonymous parallelism is seen, for example, in Luke 1:46b-47:

My soul magnifies the Lord,
and my spirit rejoices in God my Savior. . . .

The macarism (blessing) in v. 42 of the same chapter exhibits synthetic parallelism:

Blessed are you among women,
and blessed is the fruit of your womb!

Synthetic parallelism is also seen in v. 51:

He has shown strength with his arm,
he has scattered the proud in the imagination of their hearts. . . .

---

5. The discussion that begins at this point and continues to the next subheading replaces Prof. Stenger's similar discussion of Psalm 1 [trans. and ed.].

Two examples of antithetical parallelism appear in vv. 52 and 53:

> [H]e has put down the mighty from their thrones,
> and exalted those of low degree;
> he has filled the hungry with good things,
> and the rich he has sent empty away.

Both of these verses show that an aspect of antithetical parallelism is mention of what is shared (in both cases, God's action in reversing the human lot) alongside what is contrasted (the fate of rich and poor). In the antithetical parallelism in Luke 2:14 the shared element is the structure of the two clauses, and the contrasting elements are heaven and earth, glory and peace, and God and humans.

These forms of parallelism can be considered representatives of a broader range of structures involving repetition and contrast that do not all come under the heading of Hebrew parallelism.[6] Among such structures are, for instance, changes of number and chiasmus. The interplay of singular and plural in Luke 11:31f. is such a structuring element:

- the Queen of the South (singular)
- those of this generation (plural)
- the people of Nineveh (plural)
- this generation (singular).

Chiasmus is reverse parallelism. A rudimentary instance of chiasmus is seen in Luke 1:52f., quoted above as containing two examples of antithetic parallelism: The fate of those in positions of power is mentioned first and last, with the destiny of the poor named in the middle two clauses (a, b, b', a'; cf. "you — Christ — Christ — you" in Col 3:3f.).

Imagery can also be a structuring element. The exaggerated imagery of Matt 7:3-5 brings the contrasts of large (the log) and small (the speck) and second person (you) and third person (your brother) into a memorable structure. Here again, the expression of contrast involves similarity (in your/your brother's *eye*). Where particular images begin

---

6. See E. A. Nida, et al., *Style and Discourse, with Special Reference to the Text of the Greek New Testament* (Cape Town: Bible Society of South Africa, 1983) 174-81, for detailed analysis and New Testament examples of the many possible such structures.

and end often give structure to discourses, as, for example, in the parable collections (e.g., Mark 4).

Metatextual Devices and Other Text Dividers

Two other structural devices that function in both poetry and prose (whether narrative or argumentative) are *headings,* such as those that appear in 1 Corinthians (e.g., 8:1: "Now concerning . . ."),[7] and *summaries* appearing at the ends of sections. Sentences or other textual components that refer to the whole of a preceding text fulfill a similar function. For instance, in an argumentative text the author can spell out for the reader the intention of the text, as, for example, in 1 Tim 3:14f.: "I am writing these instructions to you so that . . . you may know. . . ." In a narrative text the author or a later editor may comment on the narrative in order to instruct the reader in how to understand some aspect of the story, as, for example, in John 21:23: "The saying spread abroad among the brethren that this disciple was not to die; yet Jesus did not say to him that he was not to die, but, 'If it is my will that he remain, what is that to you?'"

Such structural devices are not in themselves part of the argumentation or narrative of the texts they appear in. Rather, they are to a certain extent "metatextual" in relation to the text. They take the text itself as their subject matter, so that one can refer to them as *metanarratival* or *metaargumentative.*

Metatextual sentences also include citation formulas, that is, any clause that introduces a quotation or tradition and points out its character as a citation. Along with what is cited, such a clause can draw attention to a structurally significant transition point. The citation formula "Great indeed, as is known to all, is the mystery of our religion" in 1 Tim 3:16 introduces as a traditional confession the christological hymn that follows. This formula stands with the hymn itself at a transition point that is very significant in understanding the structure of the letter as a whole.

Headings, summaries, citation formulas, and metanarratival or

---

7. This does not include headings provided by translators (or by the editors of some editions of the Greek text) as aids to reading, which are clearly not part of the text to be interpreted.

metaargumentative sentences are all elements of the stage, so to speak, on which the play of the text itself unfolds. Related functions are carried out by elements that indicate, to extend the metaphor, changes in scene or perspective, for instance the abrupt introduction of the second person singular in Luke 1:76 ("And you, child, . . ."). Similarly, in a thanksgiving section at the beginning of most of his letters, Paul draws the reader's attention to the letter's recipients (e.g., 1 Thess 1:2ff.) and then goes on to speak of himself as the author of the letter (2:1ff.). Not until we have observed how this transition is made can we determine where the thanksgiving ends; nor can we decide where the main body of the letter begins without identifying the section focused on the author, the "epistolary self-recommendation."

Sometimes a change in subject matter occurs without being signaled by any of these devices. But it is important when possibly faced with such a situation — as always when evaluating structural elements related to content — to guard against subjective judgment and interpretation. In other words, one must be alert to see just how such a change in subject matter is signaled at what we can call the "formal" levels of language.

Some textual elements, although themselves part of the narrative or argument (rather than being metatextual), also have a role in relation to the whole of the narrative or argument and so can play a part in determining the text's structure. One can point, for instance, to the device of inclusio, which is the repetition of a word or larger element at the beginning and end of a passage to set the passage in a frame. Inclusio is particularly common in Matthew. For instance, "the kingdom of heaven" is mentioned in the first and eighth of the Beatitudes (Matt 5:3, 10). The Gospel of Mark, on the other hand, has a predilection for "sandwiching," that is, for concentric ordering of partial texts, as, for example, where he frames the story of the healing of a woman (Mark 5:25-34) with the beginning (vv. 21-24) and end (vv. 35-43) of the story of the raising of Jairus's daughter. Here again we can also mention chiasmus, which involves an inversion in the second of two parallel phrases, clauses, or other elements (e.g., Luke 1:52f.; Col 3:3f.).

Text divisions are also signaled by the use of pronouns, whether they refer back to textual elements in preceding parts of the text (and so are referred to as "anaphoric") or forward to textual elements that will follow later (and so are referred to as "kataphoric"), and by conjunctions and particles, which serve not only to relate sentences, but also to organize and structure elements at the textual level. Indeed, anything that establishes relationships among elements in a text also signals where text divisions occur.

STRUCTURES AT DIFFERENT LEVELS OF A TEXT

The attention we give at the stage of segmentation to text dividers and structural signals provides us with an initial understanding of the hierarchical organization of textual components. In a narrative text, for example, a temporal indicator may encompass a span of time that is then divided by more specific designations, which can be said to be subordinate to the broader designation. Similar hierarchical subordinations of textual components result when detailed or specific references to locations come under a broader indication of place, or when events are said to occur within a larger block of action and are differentiated from that larger block just as the individual features of a painting can be distinguished from the painting as a whole.

But though we begin to see these hierarchical interrelationships among textual components already at the stage of segmentation, we see them only as a sequence or succession of textual components. The segmented text is linear and its components are like links of a chain, even if we are aware of the relationships of those links.

But a text is not made up only of the relationships in linear succession of a set of linguistic signs or textual components. A text also involves interrelationships among these signs and textual components that transcend succession and are, so to speak, spatial. A writer does not create a true narrative text, for example, simply by arranging individual episodes in succession in a purely additive fashion, in the way children might connect events together in a series lacking any genuine connections by repeating the phrase "and then. . . ." Events appear in a genuine narrative in linear succession, but they must have something to do with one another. They must exhibit some common thread or be related to one another in what we might call the syntax of the story itself, that is, in hierarchical relationships. They must be fused into a structure within the whole of the narrative.

Structures of Narrative Texts

The simplest demonstration of this is a story in which one state of affairs is changed to another by means of an event, a turning point. With Aristotle we can refer to a narrative that ends with a negative state of affairs after beginning positively as "tragic" and to one that takes the reverse course as "comic"; this can be represented graphically in this way:

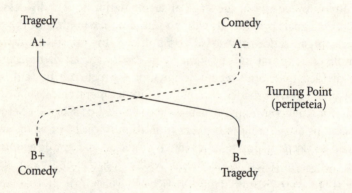

In comedy and tragedy the beginning and ending conditions (A) are opposite to each other. One need only think of the title of the novel *War and Peace,* or, to bring out the point, "War *vs.* Peace."

In a New Testament miracle story, for example, the course of events takes as its point of departure the situation of distress portrayed at the beginning of the narrative. From there it proceeds to the petition for healing and the granting of that petition in the miracle worker's words or deeds (or both) — the turning point — and then to the nonexistence of the original distress as the final state of affairs. So the story is "comic" in the technical sense of the word. The change narrated in the story also entails a change in the relationships of the characters in the story from the beginning to the end of the story.

The contrast between the circumstances of two characters also structures the text of the parable discussed above (Luke 18:9-14). Their identification already contrasts them to one another, since Pharisees were generally viewed as righteous and tax collectors as "sinners." But the parable discloses that despite this difference between the two men, before God the state of affairs is other than what is generally assumed, since the "sinner" "went down to his house justified" rather than the Pharisee. That is to say, in the course of the parable the Pharisee undergoes a "tragic" development, the tax collector in contrast a "comic" development. The similarity and contrast between the two men set the textual components in relationships of correspondence and contrast and thus constitute the parable's structure; or rather, they constitute *one* of its structures, namely, that at the level of action and actors. For like other texts, this story exhibits more than one structural level.

Another structurally significant level in our parable is seen, for example, in what the two men say. Here, too, we see both similarity and contrast. That God is addressed in both speeches makes it clear that both are prayers; this establishes their equivalence. But the two prayers stand in a relationship of contrast already at a purely quantitative level because of the Pharisee's verbosity and the tax collector's brevity. This contrast is confirmed at the level of content: The Pharisee's conceited "prayer," with its derisive and condescending attitude toward others, is contrasted to the tax collector's humble petition for forgiveness.

Among the various structural levels of a given text, one frequently exerts more influence than the others, or hierarchically sets the tone for the text. In narrative texts this dominant level is usually that of the action and actors. Thus in this parable the structure given by spatial information only supports the fundamental contrast of the characters. The Pharisee is set apart spatially, "standing" and praying "with himself," while the tax collector "stands far off" and will not so much as "lift his eyes to heaven." This spatial distinction suspends the initial unity of the place in which the two characters act out their roles, namely, the "temple."

It is striking that there are no indications of time in the parable, and that temporal structure plays no role in the text. This is in keeping with the fact that as a parable the story presents us with something that is, so to speak, of timeless validity. What is said is true also of those in the world of real life who, like the one of the characters in the narrated world of the parable, "trust in themselves that they are righteous and despise others."

This brings us to a further structural level in the parable, the level of the relationship between the narrated world of the parable and the real world of those who hear the parable. The two verses that frame the narrated world of the parable, vv. 9 and 14, address the real world of the hearers and present that real world as equivalent to the narrated world. Therefore, the judgment pronounced by Jesus over the characters in the parable is simultaneously pronounced over his listeners: "This man went home justified rather than the other."

We first set out this text (p. 30 above) by reworking the verse divisions into a more precise set of divisions. Now we can supply the text with a more sophisticated framework and designation of parts to reveal not only the text's successive textual components but also its structure of interrelated sequences (autonomous units of action) and subordinated segments (see the diagram on p. 41).

Structures of Nonnarrative Texts

In narrative texts the most significant structural elements affecting hierarchical relationships are usually found at the level of the actors and the action. But in other types of texts one can frequently identify the most significant structural elements only after repeated reading and probing. In poetic texts, for example, the interpreter must decide whether the determinative structure is parallelism, imagery, or, perhaps, characters, that is, which best enables us to understand the text's overall structure.

If we take Luke 1:51-53 as an example,[8] we see that the interactions of characters are determinative. The structures at the levels of parallelism (see above, pp. 33-34) and of imagery (e.g., "arm," heart," "thrones") are subordinated to and serve the macrostructure, that is, the overriding structure, provided by the juxtapositions of the "proud/mighty/rich" and the "humble/hungry" and of God's actions toward these two sides of humanity. The subordinate structures of parallelism and imagery provide the microstructure of these three verses of the Magnificat.

Another example is provided by Romans 13. The imagery of indebtedness, which began in v. 7, is a subordinate structure that provides the introduction to the dominant structure of the relation of the imperative of love to the Mosaic law code. The list derived from the Decalogue (v. 9) is another microstructural detail, subordinate to the statement made in two ways at the beginning, middle, and end of the passage concerning the fulfillment of the law by love.

---

8. Here, as above, discussion of two New Testament texts replaces Prof. Stenger's discussion of Psalm 1 [trans. and ed.].

Luke 18:9-14

A	9a He also told this parable to some trusting in themselves a₁ that they were righteous a and despising others:	Discourse intro-duction (from the Gospel writer)
I	10a "Two men went up to the temple to pray. b One was a Pharisee, c and the other was a tax collector.	Setting for the action
II	11a The Pharisee stood praying with himself,	Discourse introduction I
	b 'O God, c I thank you d that I am not like other people, e robbers, f unjust, g adulterers, h or even like this tax collector. 12a I fast twice a week, b I give tithes of all c that I receive.'	Discourse I
III	13a The tax collector, standing far away, would not even lift up his eyes to heaven, b but hit against his chest, saying,	Discourse introduction II
	c 'O God, d be merciful to me a sinner.'	Discourse II
	14a I tell you,	Discourse intro-duction for the story-teller's commentary
	b this man went down to his house justified rather than the other."	Storyteller's (Jesus') commentary
A′	c For everyone exalting himself will be humbled, d but the one humbling himself will be exalted.	Gospel writer's commentary

Structures and Form

As we have seen, then, different levels of structure can be distinguished in any text. The elements of each level stand in relationships of similarity and contrast and are organized in structures that the exegete must describe analytically. These levels of structure are like the transparent overlays of a multi-level map, so that their patterns are sometimes exactly the same, or can sometimes influence the reader's understanding of other levels, or can sometimes support and amplify other levels. Each level contributes to what amid all the complexity is nonetheless a unified pattern, and all the levels taken together form this pattern. The human body is also composed of various "levels," each of which constitutes an independent structure. The skeletal system is one such structural level, the vascular system a second, the lymphatic system a third, the nervous system a fourth, and so on. These various structured systems do not in every respect reflect the same pattern or structure, yet as layers of individual patterns they function together, and in and through these complex interrelationships they constitute the human body. Similarly, the various structured levels of a text constitute that text's body.

How many levels there are depends on what kind of text is being read. Poetic texts add further structural levels to those of everyday language, such as rhyme, meter, and parallelism. Some levels of language are not accessible in analysis of translated texts. For example, one gains little by focusing on the system of verb tenses in a translation, since the translator may have rendered the tenses inconsistently. But translations do to a large extent preserve such elements as direct address, the cast of characters in narrative, and spatial and temporal information. This enables the exegete to do structural analysis on the basis of a translation, particularly since structural patterns at one level (which may be lost in translation) frequently recur at another level (where they may be preserved in translation).

But in structural analysis it is essential that only one level be followed at a time and that the different levels not be mixed. One should not allow one's description of one structural level to be affected by observations made on a different level. Only after each of the various structural levels has been described independently can the exegete move on to the task of understanding their interaction. This interaction involves all the structural levels in the text, from the levels of language itself, for example, that of sound, which are still removed from any consideration of actual content, to the semantic levels of content and function. Ultimately, this interaction makes up the text's individual countenance and constitutes what we can call the *form* of a text. The task of formal analysis, broadly considered, is to describe this form. Therefore, "form" is to be distinguished from "structure," "form" referring to the result of this interplay between the structural levels of a text and "structure" referring to the textual arrangement of individual elements of a specific text in their various hierarchical relationships at only *one* of these many levels of language.

This distinction allows us a more precise understanding of the difference between form and content. The content of a text is not something poured into the form like liquid into a bottle; it is, rather, just another of the levels of language whose structure the exegete must understand through analysis. Its interaction with the structural levels that do not express content constitutes a text's form. Thus "form" and "content" do not represent simply two sides of one coin. Rather, content is related only to one part of the structural levels that together constitute the form of the text, and is a subordinate concept.

Similarly, and unlike older "form criticism," one must strictly differentiate between form and *genre*. Form is determined in relation to the individual text, while genre is determined in relation to a type of text. Such types of texts are distinguished by comparison of several individual texts with respect to their structural agreement at the various levels. Therefore, we must differentiate strictly between the methods of "form criticism," as we are using the term in this book, and "genre criticism" (in German: *Gattungskritik*). Form criticism is a synchronic process of consideration of a text's shape and structures, while genre criticism is one of the exegete's diachronic methods.

CHAPTER 5

Exegetical Methods III: Diachronic Methods

DISCERNING THE TEXT'S DISUNITY

The texts we have used thus far as examples have generally been self-contained unities with tightly woven forms and structures that one can read in one sweep with no internal interruptions. This is not, however, the case with all New Testament texts, since often multiple "authors" have produced a given text.

A story or hymn, for example, might have been passed on orally in the church as one of a group of traditions, applied to new situations as it was passed on, and thus altered. Each New Testament writer was to some extent a collector of various traditions, one who has put these traditions together into a larger whole, a Gospel, for example, reworking them and adding new material to cement them together and to apply them to yet another new situation.

A particular "text" in the New Testament can be the result of this sort of process of tradition, accumulation, and redaction. As a result it might contain identifiable tensions, which become the exegete's evidence for how the process worked in the particular instance. So we must pay attention to such tensions — that is, to repetitions, contradictions in content, seams and breaks in sentence structure or narrative action, differences of style and of linguistic usage, and elements that do not fit in the genre of the larger text[1] — in order to determine whether what

---

1. This list is adapted from one by G. Strecker that appears in G. Strecker and U. Schnelle, *Einführung in die neutestamentliche Exegese* (Göttingen, 1983) 41. Cf.

we have before us is an originally unified, coherent, and consistent text or a text that has been assembled from disparate sources. This stage of exegesis has been called "literary criticism" because, in a text constructed from pieces of different origins, we must distinguish the literary layers that can be traced back to differing times or authors.[2]

An example of the results of this stage of exegesis is given in the diagram of Mark 2:1-12 on pp. 46-47. If we read this text carefully, we notice that the healing of the paralytic begins in v. 5, but continues with the words of healing only in v. 11. Jesus interrupts his words to the scribes without finishing his sentence (v. 10) and again turns his attention to the paralytic. There is a tension here. This and other observations lead the exegete to conclude that this is not a unified text, but rather one that has been assembled from disparate sources.[3] The task at this stage is complete when we come to a conclusion regarding the text's unity — that is, its coherence — or its disunity.

TRADITION CRITICISM[4] AND SOURCE CRITICISM

The articles in a typical newspaper are assembled and arranged by an editor (or by several editors). The editor reworks each article written by

---

"Twelve Criteria of Creedal Formulae in the New Testament," in E. Stauffer, *New Testament Theology* (London: SCM, 1963) 338f.

2. *Literarkritik* is the term used by Prof. Stenger for this stage of exegesis. But since "literary criticism" has come to be used in biblical studies for something quite different, i.e., synchronic study of biblical texts in the ways that other literary texts are studied, the term is avoided here. For further discussion of use of the term, see R. N. Soulen, *Handbook of Biblical Criticism* (Atlanta: John Knox, [2]1981) 113-15. Prof. Stenger distinguishes in a footnote the identification of *Literarkritik* with source criticism from use of the term for "the investigation of internal consistency." In the latter understanding it is sometimes the case that "no attention is paid to the fact that literary criticism is fundamentally a diachronic method, and should be employed only after synchronic description of structure" [trans. and ed.].

3. Cf. R. Bultmann, *History of the Synoptic Tradition,* trans. J. Marsh (New York: Harper and Row, 1963) 14-16.

4. German scholarship uses two terms that are normally translated "tradition criticism," *Überlieferungskritik* and *Traditionskritik,* the former referring to study of the transmission of traditional materials, i.e., the *process* of tradition, and the latter to the traditional materials themselves. Here "tradition criticism" is reserved for *Überlieferungskritik,* study of the process of tradition [trans. and ed.].

Mark 2:1-12

1a	And he returned to Capernaum.
b	After some days it was reported
c	that he was at home.
2a	And so many were gathered together
b	that there was no longer room for them, not even about the door,
c	and he was preaching the word to them.
3a	And they came,
b	bringing to him a paralytic
c	carried by four men.
4a	And when they could not get near him because of the crowd,
b	they removed the roof
c	where he was;
d	and when they had made an opening,
e	they let down the pallet
f	on which the paralytic lay.
5a	And when Jesus saw their faith,
b	he said to the paralytic,
c	"My son,
d	*your sins are forgiven.*"
6a	*Now some of the scribes were sitting there,*
b	*questioning in their hearts,*
7a	*"Why does this man speak thus?*
b	*It is blasphemy!*
c	*Who can forgive sins but God alone?"*
8a	*And immediately Jesus, perceiving in his spirit*
b	*that they thus questioned within themselves,*
c	*said to them,*
9a	*"Why do you question thus in your hearts?*
b	*Which is easier, to say to the paralytic*
10a	*'Your sins are forgiven,'*
b	*or to say*
c	*'Rise, take up your pallet,*
d	*and walk'?*
e	*But that you may know*
f	*that the Son of Man has authority on earth to forgive sins . . ."*
g	*he said to the paralytic:*

11a	"I say to you,
b	rise,
c	take up your pallet,
d	and go home."
12a	And he rose,
b	and immediately took up the pallet,
c	and went out before them all;
d	so that they were all amazed
e	and glorified God, saying,
f	"We never saw anything like this!"

a reporter and each dispatch received from the wire services, eliminating something here, adding something else there, and then decides where the reworked article will appear in the finished newspaper.

Similarly, when the units of tradition regarding Jesus, the small independent narratives and groups of sayings, for instance, were finally written down in each of the Gospels, they were reworked, shortened or expanded, and then placed in their particular positions within the whole of the Gospel. Each of the Gospel writers was an editor — the term more often used is "redactor" — one who unified the material received from tradition and from written sources into a single book with particular purposes for its own situation. The newspaper analogy is limited in that the positioning of different traditions in each of the Gospels is determined by their relation to each other and to the overall purpose of the Gospel, not, as is partly the case with the articles in a newspaper, simply by their size and relative importance.

Though "tradition" and "redaction" are thus mainly of concern to the interpreter of the Gospels, the writers of the other New Testament documents all made use to some extent of traditional materials (see in particular chapter 12 below). So there, too, tradition criticism comes into play.

It is sometimes possible on the basis of the tensions in a text to see through this redactional reworking and view at least the outlines of the traditional material. In Mark 2:1-12 the tradition critic might suspect that the original source was a story dealing only with the healing of a paralytic, a story that said nothing about Jesus' authority to forgive sins. This original story appears in our diagram of this passage (pp. 46-47) in normal type. Without vv. 5d-10g the text reveals itself as a miracle story showing Jesus' power over illness.[5] The tradition critic thus tries to see the original form of a text behind its present written form and to understand the changes that the text has undergone while it was being handed on.

Sometimes the critic will be aided by the presence of more than one version of a tradition. One might, for example, begin with the final redactional form of the Beatitudes in Matthew's Sermon on the Mount and Luke's Sermon on the Plain (Matt 5:3-12; Luke 6:20-22) and try to determine the form they had in the source used by both Matthew and Luke — and then look even further back to the form the Beatitudes had as words spoken by Jesus (see chapter 14 below).

In the case of the Beatitudes, the question posed by *tradition criticism* is connected to a broader question of *source criticism*, since further study shows that the Beatitudes were already, before the Gospel writers made use of them, part of a larger source, apparently a written source, consisting of sayings and discourses of Jesus (but little, if any, narrative material). The existence in some form or other of this source, which is called "Q" (from German *Quelle*, "source"), has come to be a relatively stable working hypothesis of most Gospel interpreters. In composing their Gospels, Matthew and Luke drew material from both Q and the Gospel of Mark. Q is the source in most of those instances where Matthew and Luke agree in material not represented in Mark. Source criticism has thus led to what is known as the basic "two-source theory" regarding the sources of Matthew and Luke.[6]

Source criticism is more difficult where only one form of a text can be taken as the point of departure for a differentiation of sources.

---

5. In regard to genre, this traditional piece is a story of miraculous healing. There are, of course, many examples of this genre in the New Testament. What sets this story apart from others of its genre is the determination of the paralytic's helpers, which the tradition calls "faith" (Mark 2:5a).

6. The two-document hypothesis has undergone several refinements, the best-known in the English-speaking world being the four-document hypothesis, which adds to Q and Mark sources used only by Matthew and only by Luke ("M" and "L," respectively). The classic statement of the four-document hypothesis is B. H. Streeter's *The Four Gospels: A Study in Origins* (London: Macmillan, 1924). For a view of some of the variety in Synoptic source criticism, see H. C. Kee, "Synoptic Studies," in *The New Testament and its Modern Interpreters*, ed. E. J. Epp and G. W. Macrae (Philadelphia: Fortress: 1989) 245-69; cf. n. 10 below. On the history of Synoptic source criticism see W. G. Kümmel, *Introduction to the New Testament* (trans. H. C. Kee; Nashville: Abingdon, [2]1975) 44-52.

Nonetheless, the tensions, redundancies, and contradictions in texts enable us to reconstruct, for example, what has become known as the "signs source" used in the Gospel of John and to distinguish it from the redactional material that it has been imbedded in.[7] The case is similar for Mark. Critics assume that the writer of Mark not only used individual traditions passed down to him, but also occasionally drew on larger bodies of material that had already been committed to written form, for example, in the Passion account.[8]

In dealing with tradition criticism and source criticism, students are generally dependent on what scholars have already published in introductions to the New Testament and the standard commentaries,[9] even more than they are in regard to form criticism. A growing understanding of these stages of exegesis and a developing independence in applying them are essential for the exegete. But that the experts often disagree in regard to the results of their source-critical work[10] is a reminder that we need to be cautious in our espousal of any particular hypothesis.

REDACTION CRITICISM

Redaction criticism is, in relation to tradition criticism, the other side of the same coin. It attempts to identify elements in a text that can be traced back to the redactor, that is, to the person who received and redactionally reworked the traditional materials and sources. Earlier scholars considered the participation of the redactor in the finished text as insignificant, limited primarily to the conservation and handing on

---

7. See R. Bultmann, *The Gospel of John: A Commentary,* trans. G. R. Beasley-Murray, et al. (Philadelphia: Westminster, 1971) 6f. ("miracle-source"); R. E. Brown, *The Gospel according to John* (Anchor Bible; Garden City, NY: Doubleday, 1966) I, xxix.

8. Two source-critical studies of Mark are found in, e.g., H.-W. Kuhn, *Ältere Sammlungen im Markusevangelium* (Göttingen: Vandenhoeck & Ruprecht, 1971), and E. Trocmé, *The Formation of the Gospel according to Mark,* trans. P. Gaughan (Philadelphia: Fortress, 1975).

9. See the bibliography at the end of this book, especially pp. 176 and 178-79.

10. The most obvious example on the source-critical level is the challenge to the Mark-Q two-source hypothesis by scholars who regard Matthew, not Mark, as the earliest-written Gospel. See Kee, "Synoptic Studies," 248-51 for discussion of this view.

of what was received. But redaction criticism has taught us to view the redactors of the biblical books as writers and theologians in their own right. They not only transmitted the traditions by arranging and re-working them, but as theological writers in their own right they also recast what they received to say something within their own situations.

Like tradition criticism, redaction criticism is based on the tensions, redundancies, and interruptions in the text that allow us to differentiate redaction from tradition. The criteria for this differentiation include the redactor's style, use of language, favored theological themes, and compositional technique. A concordance is an indispensable tool for this work. By comparing the frequency of particular words in different texts, the exegete is able to identify the words, themes, and concepts favored or avoided by particular New Testament writers and then to identify their use in given contexts with particular stages of transmission or redaction. Needless to say, this is best done in Greek,[11] but steps can be taken in understanding how tradition and redaction are discerned by using a concordance to an English translation, especially if it is keyed to the Greek.[12]

In Mark 2:1-12, for example, we suspect that the Gospel writer introduced the theme of Jesus' forgiveness of sins (the verses printed in italics in the diagram on p. 46). The tension that arises from Jesus' mid-sentence interruption of his speech to the scribes shows that the Gospel writer still wanted the older narrative of miraculous healing to

---

11. Concordances of the Greek text include W. F. Moulton, A. S. Geden, and H. K. Moulton, *A Concordance to the Greek Testament* (Edinburgh: Clark, [5]1978), and *Concordance to the Novum Testamentum Graece of Nestle-Aland, 26th Edition, and to the Greek New Testament, 3rd Edition* (Berlin and New York: de Gruyter, [3]1987).

12. E.g., R. E. Whitaker, *The Eerdmans Analytical Concordance to the Revised Standard Version of the Bible* (Grand Rapids: Eerdmans, 1988). Dictionaries of New Testament words also usually list the passages in which individual words occur and then go beyond that to discuss the usage and history of each word. The most easily accessible such work for the student with little or no Greek is *The New International Dictionary of New Testament Theology*, ed. C. Brown (3 vols.; Grand Rapids: Zondervan, 1967-78). Two that contain English indexes are the *Theological Dictionary of the New Testament*, ed. G. Kittel and G. Friedrich, trans. G. W. Bromiley (10 vols.; Grand Rapids: Eerdmans, 1964-76) and the *Exegetical Dictionary of the New Testament*, ed. H. Balz and G. Schneider (3 vols.; Grand Rapids: Eerdmans, 1990-93), though to use them one should probably at least know the Greek alphabet. The standard lexicon of New Testament Greek is by W. Bauer, adapted for English readers by W. F. Arndt, F. W. Gingrich, and F. Danker as *A Greek-English Lexicon of the New Testament and Other Early Christian Literature* (Chicago: University of Chicago, [2]1979).

be completed. The writer uses the traditional story to show the inbreaking of God's healing power into the world through Jesus. With his addition to the story he shows that God's healing power in Jesus seeks to deliver people from what cripples them most, which is sin.

The writer not only alters the text that was handed down but also assigns that text its place in the whole of the document that is being written. Therefore, the redaction critic is also concerned with where a given text falls in the document and, beyond that, with how the whole document has been structured.[13]

If, for example, we look at the context of Mark 2:1-12, we find that the Gospel writer uses it to open a series of five texts (2:1-12, 13-17, 18-22, 23-28; 3:1-6) in which Jesus' opponents invariably take offense at his behavior or his disciples' behavior, and in each case his response shows that they are in the wrong. This series of texts concludes with the sentence: "The Pharisees went out, and immediately held counsel with the Herodians against him, how to destroy him." The arrangement of these texts resulted from the Gospel writer's own intentions, which were to show, near the beginning of the Gospel, that from the very outset God's offer of life in Jesus faced opposition.[14]

THE ELEMENTS OF TRADITIONS[15]

Tradition criticism, as described above, deals with the small, relatively self-contained units of tradition passed down to the New Testament authors and incorporated into their writings, for instance, the account of a particular miraculous healing as in Mark 2:1-12. The redaction

13. In this subsection Prof. Stenger distinguishes between *Redaktionskritik* and *Kompositionskritik*, but both tasks have usually come under the term "redaction criticism" in the English-speaking world [trans. and ed.].

14. Strictly speaking, one can speak of *diachronic* redaction criticism focusing on the arrangement of texts only when one can determine that the redactor has altered the arrangement present in a source and has thus also altered the source's meaning by rearranging the texts. An analysis that establishes a text's meaning only from observation of its present macrostructure is not diachronic, but synchronic. As such, we should consider such work an aspect of form criticism, except that the "form" is not a partial text but rather a self-contained text, that is, in this case, an entire Gospel.

15. Prof. Stenger's title for this section is *Traditionskritik*. See n. 4 above [trans. and ed.].

critic looks in one direction, at how this unit of tradition is used by the Gospel writer in building the story of Jesus told in the particular Gospel.

If we look the other direction, so to speak, we can seek to identify and describe the conventional schemata of thought and expression, which are called "topoi" (singular "topos"), that lie below the level of the units of tradition that we have identified in New Testament texts. These topoi are the fixed formulas, themes, concepts, metaphors, and motifs that work as the building blocks of tradition, though they are not independent units of tradition themselves.[16]

A motif, for instance, is a typical situation that can become the motivating element in several narratives, as, for example, the motif of the "adversarial brothers" functions similarly in several stories in Genesis (chs. 4, 25, 32f., 37, 42ff.) or as the fundamental outline of healing stories functions again and again in New Testament narrative texts. Among the metaphors also shared by different texts and units of tradition are, for example, numerous terms for human relationships, such as "brother," used as a term for fellow Christians (e.g., 1 Cor 1:1) and "bride of Christ" as a designation for the church (John 3:29; 2 Cor 11:2; Rev 19, 21–22). Fixed themes and symbols appear in frequently occurring combinations of words such "the righteousness of God" or "the day of the Lord." Other consistent combinations of words include formulaic phrases such as the reference to God as the one who "raised Jesus from the dead" (e.g., Rom 10:9; 1 Cor 15:15; 1 Cor 6:14; 1 Thess 1:9f.).

These basic elements of tradition are not what we call units of tradition. They are, rather, the basic elements out of which the traditions are built. Therefore, attention to them enables us to understand the background and function of the units of tradition in the different contexts they find themselves in their transmission and redaction.

Genre Criticism

Structures and Histories of Genres

Whereas form criticism is concerned with understanding and describing the shape of a specific text, genre criticism looks at what is shared by a

---

16. See the fuller definition in Soulen, *Handbook* 199.

number of texts.[17] Specifically, it aims at grouping the particular text with structurally identical or similar texts and thereby at understanding that text together with the others as members of a family that thus share a structural pattern. The structural pattern does not exist on its own; it is rather an abstraction established by comparison of several structurally similar texts.

Genre criticism is related to tradition criticism in that both deal with fixed materials. But genre criticism focuses on the hierarchically determinative structure of a text, on the assumption that the text follows a structure that is also at work in other texts, a structure discernible in the typical features characteristic of that particular genre.

We have identified the story of the healing of the paralytic in Mark 2 as a unit of tradition. With respect to genre, it belongs among stories portraying miraculous healings. Its narrative follows the structure common to miracle stories in general and to miraculous healings of paralytics in particular. Pesch enumerates the following structural characteristics of this genre:[18]

1. the presence of the miracle worker and of a crowd (introductory and preparatory motifs, vv. 1-2),
2. the encounter of the miracle worker with the ill or disabled person, whose sickness or distress is portrayed (v. 3),
3. difficulties in the way of this encounter (this stage replaces the traditional plea for healing) that must be overcome (v. 4),
4. the action of healing by means of a vocative and a promise (v. 5) and the word of healing, the command for action demonstrating the healing, and the dismissal (v. 11),
5. confirmation of the healing (v. 12),
6. demonstration of the healing (v. 12),
7. astonishment on the part of the crowd (v. 12), and
8. the crowd's concluding remark (v. 12).

The genre-critical procedure thus confirms our earlier tradition-critical hypothesis: The text we established as the unit of tradition corresponds to the structural pattern of the genre, and the textual components we identified as later additions interrupt the typical pattern for the genre.

---

17. "Genre" is used throughout this book for German *Gattung* [trans. and ed.].
18. R. Pesch, *Das Markusevangelium* (HTKNT; Freiburg: Herder, 1976) I, 152f.

Genre criticism belongs to the diachronic methods of exegesis because the texts used to establish the typical features of a genre come from different times. Therefore, genre criticism goes beyond comparison of individual representatives of a genre to a reconstruction of the history of the genre. Our knowledge of early church history is thus expanded in that it comes to include the history of the different ways in which the church expressed itself.

Distinguishing Genres

Genres do not exist in reality in any concrete sense, but are, rather, established through a process of abstraction: Certain features of a given text prove to be characteristic of its genre, while other features are not. Because it stands for a series of abstractions, the term "genre" exhibits a certain degree of ambiguity, which is reflected in the multiplicity of genre designations. Many different ways of classifying and naming New Testament genres have been proposed.

Genres are discovered only empirically, that is, by reading the New Testament texts themselves. Reading one text facilitates the reading of others, which facilitates the reading of others, and so on, so that the texts arrange themselves seemingly "on their own" in groups of structurally related texts. But in the face of the disorganized multiplicity of texts and possible genre types, we must accept, at least provisionally, the categories of texts discovered by earlier readers, allowing them to "presort" for us the vast multiplicity of texts and genres, even if we know this is not an arrangement with any "finality." And we must keep in mind that the practical goal of genre criticism is neither a timeless system nor an endless list of genres, which in the final analysis would only end up equating genre with individual text, since every text bears some differences from every other text.

Theissen's suggestions with regard to the genres of traditions in the Synoptic Gospels exemplify this practical ideal.[19] He distinguishes four basic genres in the Synoptic material from "pure teaching" to "narrative teaching" to "narrative with a didactic point" to "pure narrative," or, using the traditional terminology of New Testament

19. G. Theissen, *The Miracle Stories of the Early Christian Tradition*, trans. F. McDonagh (Philadelphia: Fortress, 1982) 119f.

scholars, "logia, parables, apophthegms [i.e., biographical narratives with didactic purposes], and narratives." He then makes distinctions within each of these four basic genres according to the polarity of "typical" vs. "particular."

Sayings (logia), for instance, can be "normative" or "kerygmatic." "Normative sayings" are those that address "what is universally valid in experience or action: wisdom sayings, legal sayings and community rules." They are "concerned with rules of experience or action, with what is normal and typical." "Kerygmatic sayings," on the other hand, are those that "announce or proclaim a particular event, an event which has already taken place (I-sayings, Son of Man sayings) or is in the process of taking place or . . . is to take place in the future (prophetic and apocalyptic sayings)." Kerygmatic sayings "always contain a message about a particular. They interpret the present and unveil the future."

Among parables, those that are "similes in the strict sense" depict "typical events" and "appeal to general experience." Other parables depict atypical, perhaps even improbable, events.

> Apophthegms can be divided similarly. Most are attempts to present the teaching of Jesus, that is, not just what he said at a particular place, but his general teaching on problems raised. In contrast to these discourses and disputes are [strictly] biographical apophthegms, which set out to portray a singular event in the life of Jesus — for example Peter's messianic confession.

Among "purely narrative genres," "miracle stories recount typical elements of the life of Jesus," as is seen where Jesus' healing power is described in summary statements (e.g., Mark 4:10-12). The miracles "are interchangeable episodes and have no fixed position in the sequence of Jesus' life." But the "legendary reports" of, for example, Jesus' birth, temptation, and Passion, "report events which have an unchangeable position in the temporal sequence of Jesus' life."[20]

Theissen summarizes all this in a diagram (somewhat amplified here):[21]

20. Ibid.
21. Ibid., 121.

typical	normative sayings	similes	discourses and disputes	miracle stories
	pure teaching	narrative teaching	narrative with a didactic point	pure narrative
particular	kerygmatic sayings	parables	biographical apophthegms	legendary reports

TEACHING (top)

NARRATIVE (bottom)

Setting in the Life of the Church and Redactional Setting

Genre criticism also includes the question of the "setting in life" (often referred to with the German phrase *Sitz im Leben*) of a given genre. The texts sharing a particular structural pattern — a particular genre — have a particular function in the life of the community that makes use of that genre. The "setting in life" of a genre is the recurring situation in the life of the community in which that genre is typically used. Wedding songs are heard at weddings, and funeral orations at funerals. "Setting in life" thus does not refer to a specific historical situation, as in, for instance, the life of Jesus. It is, rather, a sociological term, one that presupposes a community and the regular use of the texts of a specific genre in recurring situations within the life of a community.

In general, one can say that the "setting in life" of the miracle stories (including the original tradition of the healing of the paralytic) can be found in the missionary exigencies in the life of the early church. They serve the missionary proclamation by portraying Christ as the Lord and as the man of God who is able to exercise determinative power in the most diverse situations of human distress, to whom one may therefore surrender oneself in faith.

Even though genre criticism functions diachronically in its attempt to establish genre types on the basis of various individual texts that originated at different times, its results bring it back to the synchronic methods of form criticism. The genre established by genre criticism can serve form criticism as a kind of foil, the background against which the individual text acquires sharper contours.

The individual characteristics of the final redactional form of Mark 2:1-12, to refer again to our sample text, emerge with particular clarity before the background of the genre of miraculous healings. Where the plea for healing normally stands in such stories, this story reports the unusual method by which the paralytic gained access to Jesus, a method that changed an initial impossibility into a possibility and that Jesus interpreted as faith (vv. 4-5a). Furthermore, although the genre of miracle stories is indeed characterized by the miracle worker's assurance to the petitioner, the manner in which the redactor here particularizes this typical feature is very unusual: "Only here is a petitioner in a miracle story granted forgiveness of sins."[22] These two characteristics of the particular story, the single-minded faith of the helpers, who scale the roof to bring their friend to Jesus, and Jesus' ability to effect restorative change at the most profound and hidden levels of human distress, are thus thrown into relief against the background of the typical features of the genre.

Thus an examination of the story's genre not only confirms the tradition-critical hypothesis but also facilitates our form-critical understanding of the individual text. Against the background of the genre's pattern, we see all the more clearly how the function of this unit of tradition is changed by its redactional expansion. Beyond its "setting in life" it thus acquires a "setting in literature," that is, in the Gospel of Mark. As it stands in Mark, this miracle story is the framework for the offense the Pharisees take at Jesus' forgiveness of sins. This redactional use of the story breaks the connection between Jesus' assurance and his word of healing in the original miracle story. The assurance, "my son, your sins are forgiven," which provokes the Pharisees' ire in the first place, and Jesus' word of healing, "rise, take up your pallet, and go home," now become a demonstration of the fact that "the Son of man has authority on earth to forgive sins" (v. 10) and a refutation of the

22. Pesch, *Markusevangelium* I, 147.

charge of blasphemy. The contrast between the crowd and the Pharisees is created by the fact that Jesus was "preaching the word" to the crowd at the outset (which may also be a redactional addition to the story), and then at the conclusion of the text the crowd is amazed and praises God. When one group listens to Jesus, his miraculous deed moves them to praise God; the other group accuses him of blasphemy. Jesus prompts every person to make a choice.

This concludes our intentionally brief discussion of the various methods of New Testament exegesis, which has prepared the way for the following discussions of how particular texts are treated according to these methods. The different sample texts will call on us to concentrate sometimes on one method, sometimes on another. Some texts are analyzed more intensively from a form-critical perspective, while in others diachronic analysis is emphasized. Occasionally we will have the opportunity to complement or deepen the general methodological presentations that have been made.

No claim can be made that the choice of texts is "complete" from a systematic perspective. They were chosen because they have all proven to be useful for the purpose they are put here, which is to give practice in the application of the exegetical methods we have been explaining. From the perspective of source criticism, the choice of texts represents all the possibilities of Synoptic exegesis envisioned by the two-source hypothesis. Thus, we have examples from the Markan tradition and from Q and one from the Johannine "signs" tradition. The genres of lists and christological hymns also have their place, as do the Pauline letters, represented by the letter to Philemon.

An introduction to exegetical methods cannot also be an introduction to New Testament history and cultural background, to the literary characteristics of individual New Testament books, or to their particular theologies. But these areas must sometimes be addressed in exegesis of particular texts, and are addressed on occasion in the discussions that follow, and the reader should always be aware of the need for acquaintance with such concerns. Your goal should be to feel so at home in the world of the New Testament that with the help of the exegetical methods you are able to move about freely as a reader who does not need to rely completely on anyone else, a reader who can "read well." The bibliography in the last chapter of this book is intended to provide some help in moving toward this goal.

PART TWO

NEW TESTAMENT EXEGESIS
IN PRACTICE

CHAPTER 6

Jesus Calls Levi and Eats with Tax Collectors (Mark 2:13-17; Matt 9:9-13; Luke 5:27-32)

This textual unit is preserved in a threefold tradition, that is, in all three Synoptics (Mark, Matthew, Luke). Here, however, we will limit our discussion to the version which the two-source hypothesis identifies as primary, namely, the Markan version. But it will be worthwhile to examine the differences in the text as it stands in Matthew and Luke using a synopsis of the Gospels.[1]

We can easily determine the beginning and end of the textual unit. The healing of the paralytic (Mark 2:1-12) ends in the way typical of its genre, with a choral conclusion (v. 12). V. 13 introduces a change in location: "He went out again beside the sea," providing a transition to the new unit. Jesus' own words conclude the unit (v. 17), and v. 18 introduces new characters. Hence the text to be considered is Mark 2:13-17.

THE FORM OF THE TEXT

The Macrostructure

A change of location occurs at v. 13 ("he went out again beside the sea"), marking the beginning of the text. A new character is introduced in v. 14

---

1. Such a tool should be used whenever one is working with a Synoptic passage. The standard synopses in English are *Synopsis of the Four Gospels*, ed. K. Aland (New York: American Bible Society, [9]1987), and *Gospel Parallels: A Synopsis of the First Three Gospels*, ed. B. H. Throckmorton (Nashville: Nelson, [3]1967).

Mark 2:13-17

13a	He went out again beside the sea;
b	and all the crowd gathered about him,
c	and he taught them.
14a	And as he passed on,
b	he saw Levi the son of Alphaeus
c	sitting at the tax office,
d	and he said to him,
e	"Follow me."
f	And he rose
g	and followed him.
15a	And it happened
b	that as he sat at table in his house,
c	many tax collectors and sinners were sitting with Jesus and his disciples;
d	for there were many,
e	and they followed him.
16a	And when the scribes of the Pharisees saw
b	that he was eating with sinners and tax collectors
c	they said to his disciples,
d	"Why does he eat with tax collectors and sinners?"
17a	And Jesus heard it,
b	and he said to them,
c	"Those who are well have no need of a physician, but those who are sick;
d	I came not to call the righteous, but sinners."

("Levi the son of Alphaeus"), so that the first break in the text occurs after v. 13. V. 15 also introduces a change in location ("in his house") and new characters ("many tax collectors and sinners" and "his disciples"), so the second break occurs between vv. 14 and 15. More new characters come on the scene in v. 16 ("the scribes of the Pharisees"), so another break occurs between vv. 15 and 16. Since the narrative is exchanged for dialogue at v. 16, it is there that the main break of the textual unit occurs.

The Microstructure

We can further subdivide the individual textual components. V. 14 is subdivided into the sequence of the directive to follow Jesus (a-e) and its execution (f-g). A lower-level break also occurs in v. 15, since d-e ("for there were many, and they followed him") does not really "narrate," but rather offers a commentary on the narrative. The dialogue (vv. 16-17) should be subdivided because of the change in speakers from "the scribes of the Pharisees" (v. 16) to "Jesus" in v. 17. Finally, Jesus' response is subdivided into a metaphor (c) and its application (d).

ARE THERE TENSIONS IN THE TEXT?

At this stage we can examine the text with regard to internal continuity (consistency or coherence) and discontinuity (inconsistency or incoherence). On this basis we will be able to decide whether it is homogeneous in its origin or has been pieced together from heterogeneous units.

Coherence

The exhortation to follow Jesus (v. 14e) is followed compellingly by its actual execution (v. 14f-g). Furthermore, it makes sense for the utterances of the "scribes of the Pharisees" (v. 16) to be followed by Jesus' response (v. 17). And the individual textual components are also interrelated within the whole text: The catchword "call" in Jesus' response (v. 17d) echoes the call issued in v. 14e. Vv. 14 and 15 can be connected similarly: The phrase "and they followed him" in the comment in v. 15e clearly recalls the statement "and followed him" in v. 14g. Finally, the tax collector called in v. 14 participates in the meal with Jesus reported in v. 15.

The shared meal is also what ultimately connects v. 15 (or the entire narrative in vv. 14-15) with the dialogue in vv. 16-17, since it is Jesus' table fellowship with tax collectors and sinners that offends the scribes (v. 16). This relationship is supported by the fact that the scribes direct their objections to Jesus' "disciples" (v. 16), since v. 15 introduces Jesus' "disciples" as further participants at the meal. Finally, the overall cohesiveness of vv. 14-17 is supported since it is a "tax collector" who is called in v. 14 and then joined in v. 15 by additional "tax collectors and sinners," who then appear again in v. 16 ("sinners" are also mentioned in v. 17).[2] We can illustrate these elements of the text that contribute to its consistency in this diagram:

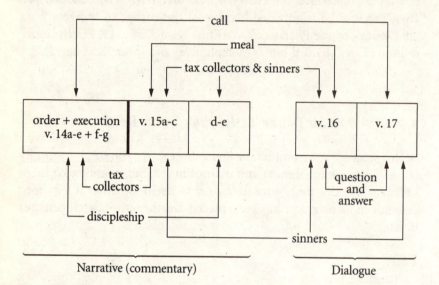

Inconsistencies

This text also exhibits certain tensions, oddities, and redundancies that generate an element of inconsistency, making our reading of the text somewhat uneven. Vv. 14-17 are closely related, but nothing relates v. 13 to what follows except that in both places Jesus is the main character. In vv. 14-17 neither the "sea" nor the "crowd" that Jesus teaches in v. 13 plays any role. Neither Jesus' name nor the content of his teaching is

---

2. The positions of "tax collectors" and "sinners" in vv. 15-16 form a chiasmus, which is itself framed by the "tax collector" in v. 14 and the "sinners" in Jesus' response (v. 17):

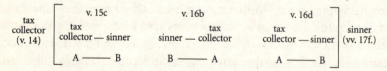

According to the rules of ancient rhetoric, chiasmus served to enclose textual elements and thus hold them together. It is quite plausible that the "author" of this text consciously employed this technique in order to support the text's consistency.

mentioned in v. 13, and that "*he* went out *again* beside the *sea*" connects this verse to what precedes, not to what follows.

V. 14 also does not include the name "Jesus." The name comes first only in v. 15, which also introduces Jesus' disciples.

V. 15 provides a transition from the narrative itself to a commentary on it. In v. 15c we learn for the first time that the tax collector Levi is surrounded by "many tax collectors and sinners," and v. 15d repeats the "many." Another redundancy occurs in this verse with "as he sat at table" (b) and "many tax collectors and sinners were sitting with Jesus and his disciples" (c); although two different Greek verbs are used, they are basically synonymous. It is not said whose "house" the meal takes place in, Jesus' or Levi's (cf. Mark and Luke).

We encounter another redundancy in v. 16 (one corrected by Matthew and Luke): Initially we are told that "the scribes of the Pharisees *saw* that he was eating with sinners and tax collectors," and then they *say* exactly the same thing in direct speech to his disciples, though with a reversal in the sequence of the two groups that Jesus is said to be eating with.

So, despite the text's fundamental consistency, the oddities and tensions it exhibits suggest that we might at least be dealing with a text that has been put together from heterogeneous elements. This suspicion deepens when tradition-critical and redaction-critical considerations suggest persuasive explanations both for the text's tensions and for its inner connections.

TRADITION AND REDACTION CRITICISM

The relatively loose connection between v. 13 and vv. 14-17 can be easily explained: V. 13 is a redactional transition constructed by the Markan redactor to connect vv. 14-17 with what precedes. Both the setting by the sea and the mention of Jesus' teaching with no indication of the content of that teaching are typical Markan characteristics, which can be confirmed by use of a concordance. And Jesus' name is not used, since it is clear from what precedes that he is the main character.

The call of Levi (v. 14) could actually stand as an autonomous, independent unit. It is shaped like other call stories and so is a member of the genre of such stories. The only element witnessing against its autonomy is that here, too, Jesus' name is not mentioned; the reader knows who the main character is only if the scene is part of a larger context. But this difficulty is resolved if originally, that is, in pre-Markan tradition, this was not the first call story of a group of such stories that were transmitted together in tradition, but rather the third, coming after the call of Simon and Andrew (1:16-18), where Jesus' name *is* mentioned, and the call of James and John (Mark 1:19-20).

"Sitting" is referred to twice because v. 15a-b, "and it happened that as he sat at table in his house," is a redactional connection of two independent traditions, the call of Levi and the meal with the tax collectors. The commentary in v. 15d-e, "for there were many, and they followed him," also clearly serves this redactional purpose: First, the repeated reference to "many" (d) explains how the individual tax collector Levi of the call story has become one of the "many tax collectors and sinners" participating in the meal. Second, "and they followed him" explains that the "many" follow Jesus just as the one tax collector of the call story followed him.

The redactional insertion of v. 15d-e necessitates the repetition of "eat with tax collectors and sinners" in v. 16, since the transition of v. 15d from narrative to commentary makes it necessary to refer back again to the meal originally related in v. 15, that is, to pick up the narrative thread again. If we omit the remark in v. 15d, we see clearly that the original sentence, "Many tax collectors and sinners were sitting at table with Jesus and his disciples," can be followed quite smoothly by "and when the scribes of the Pharisees saw *it*, they said to his disciples, 'Why does he eat with tax collectors and sinners?'"

We thus distinguish between tradition and redaction and assume the existence of two units, each originally transmitted by itself: a *call story* about the tax collector Levi, and an account of a *disputation*, telling of a meal that Jesus and his disciples shared with tax collectors and sinners. In the dispute, this meal becomes the occasion of the offense taken by the Pharisees. This offense in its own turn then precipitates Jesus' concluding response (v. 17). Thus the tensions and redundancies in the present text can be explained as having been caused by the redaction, which fused the call story and the disputation into a new textual unit.

The assumption of redactional alterations also explains some of the elements we found contributing to the present text's coherence. In the call story, it is a tax collector who is called; this makes it possible for the redactor to use the call story to anticipate the disputation concerning the meal with tax collectors. In v. 15b the redactor emphasizes that the tax collectors eating with Jesus followed him. This means, however, that the redactor has them come to the meal only as a result of following Jesus, as did Levi. At a redactional level, then, this answers the question of how Jesus came to share table fellowship with tax collectors and sinners in the first place. If we were to read the account of the dispute about table fellowship without the redactional connection of it to the call of the tax collector Levi, we would have to conclude that Jesus sought out the company of tax collectors and sinners, and this would have considerable consequences for our understanding of the earthly Jesus. But the redactor alleviates somewhat the controversial nature of this understanding of Jesus by prefacing the dispute with the call story; thus the reader must come away with the impression that Jesus also called the tax collectors and sinners who are participating in the meal, and that they, too, followed Jesus, as did Levi.

This also clarifies on one level the question concerning whose house was the setting of the meal: Since the tax collectors and sinners followed Jesus, it is clear on the level of the redaction that it is Jesus' house that is intended. This idea comes up again in the second part of Jesus' response, which in the present context clearly refers back to the call of Levi: "I came not to call the righteous, but sinners" (v. 17d). Since this sentence echoes the call story, we are justified in thinking that it, too, is redactional, and that the disputation originally concluded with the metaphorical statement that "those who are well have no need of a physician, but those who are sick" (v. 17c).

GENRE CRITICISM

The Structure of the Genre

Our discussion of tradition and redaction criticism has prompted us to conclude that in a pre-Markan stage the call of Levi (Mark 2:14) followed the call stories of Simon and Andrew (1:16-18) and James and John (1:19-20). Structurally, at least, these three stories are similar enough to suggest that they share the same genre.

Mark 1:16-20

16a	And passing along by the Sea of Galilee,
b	he saw Simon and Andrew the brother of Simon
c	casting a net in the sea;
d	for they were fishermen.
17a	And Jesus said to them,
b	"Here!
c	Follow me!
d	And I will make you
e	become fishers for people."
18a	And immediately they left their nets
b	and followed him.
19a	And going on a little farther,
b	he saw James the son of Zebedee and John his brother,
c	who were in their boat
d	mending their nets.
20a	And immediately he called them;
b	and they left their father Zebedee in the boat with the hired servants
c	and followed him.

Specifically, first of all, all five of the men that Jesus calls are mentioned by name and all but one, Simon, are identified by some family relationship as well (1:16b, 19b; 2:14b). That James and John are Zebedee's sons (v. 19b) is important for the continuity of their story, since Zebedee, whom they leave behind "in the boat with the hired servants" (v. 20b), is part of the past life that they leave to follow Jesus. In the case of Simon and Andrew, on the other hand, it is the "nets" (v. 18a) that represent their past, specifically, their previous profession.

It is as Jesus is passing by that he encounters these five men, all of them while they are engaged in their work. His exhortation to "follow" him is in the form of direct speech (1:17; 2:14) or indirect speech (1:20). The three kinds of work represented are simple professions, or professions held in low esteem, which throws some light on the environment from which the early Christians came.

In each case we hear not only what these men leave behind, but also that they "followed him," that is, Jesus. The call of Simon and James is unique in that it indicates a goal of the call: "I will make you fishers for people." In this case, the new life initiated by the call continues the previous activity in a sense, but on a different plane. In the other cases the goal of the call and of the response to it emerges from the context.

With Levi this context is redactional: Jesus' meal with the tax collectors and sinners suggests that the goal of Levi's calling and following is fellowship with Jesus. This redactional context has Jesus say that he has not come to call the righteous, but rather sinners. Again, redactional manipulation of the context now presents Levi as one of these "sinners." Though we still see dimly here that the call and the following involve a new existence for the person called, the redactional alteration of the context conceals the fact that the genre of call story is primarily concerned with the installation of a person in an office. In this way the call story genre resembles the genre of prophetic calling (e.g., Isaiah 40:1-8), though in the latter it is generally God himself who calls, whereas in the call story it is a human being.

The History of the Genre

This element of new existence and calling to an office is even more pronounced in the story of the call of Elisha (1 Kings 19:19-21), which is thus like the story of Simon and Andrew. Elisha's story does exhibit an adapted form of the characteristic feature of the genre of "prophetic call," namely, that the person called objects to the calling itself.

But we can easily see in the account of Elisha's call features found in the New Testament call stories: The person called is identified by name and family and is called while he is engaged in his profession, which is one that is not ranked very high on the social scale. But the call itself is not spoken, as in the New Testament stories, but is given by a gesture: Elijah throws his mantle — representing the prophetic office — over Elisha and thus calls him to be his follower and designates him as the future prophet (1 Kings 19:19). In contrast to the New Testament stories we have examined (but not in others: cf. Matt 8:21-22; Luke 9:59-62), the one called seeks to postpone his response: Instead of immediately heeding the call, Elisha asks permission to say goodbye to his parents before commencing with his apprenticeship to Elijah (v. 20). Elisha's response to Elijah's rejection of this request is a sign of his radical departure from his previous life: He prepare a farewell meal from the flesh of the oxen he had been plowing with, cooked over their burning yoke.

If we compare this text with structurally similar ones, we can easily discern the genre pattern of the "call story" in all its details: The person issuing the call passes by the person to be called, who is introduced by name and family and who is said to be engaged in his ordinary profession. The person giving the call does so by means of either words or gestures. After a request for postponement, which is rejected, the person called leaves behind his previous life and existence and heeds the exhortation to follow. The initiative always lies with the person giving the call. It is thus not surprising that in stories where the initiative is taken by a potential disciple (Mark 10:17-22; Matt 8:19-20), that person does not actually end up following.[3]

3. This genre pattern of the biblical call story is rigid enough to be discernible when it recurs in modern literature in an altered form. One of Franz Kafka's diary entries (July 29, 1917) contains this story (*The Diaries of Franz Kafka 1914-23*, trans. M. Greenberg with H. Arendt, ed. M. Brod [New York: Schocken, 1949] 170-71):

> Our King made no display of pomp; anyone who did not know him from his pictures would never have recognized him as the King. His clothes were badly made, not in our shop, however, of a skimpy material, his coat forever unbuttoned, flapping, and wrinkled, his hat crumpled, clumsy, heavy boots, broad, careless movements of his arms, a strong face with a large, straight, masculine nose, a short moustache, dark, somewhat too sharp eyes, a powerful, well-shaped neck. Once he stopped in passing in the doorway of our shop, put his right hand up against the lintel of the door, and asked, "Is Franz here?" He knew everyone by name. I came out of my dark corner and made my way through the journeymen. "Come along," he said, after briefly glancing at me. "He's moving into the castle," he said to the master.

This text begins, unlike the biblical call-stories, with an extended description of the person giving the call. From this description we learn — again, unlike the biblical stories — that the person called already knows the "king," either from pictures or from having seen him personally.

But the second part of the text, the actual story itself (from "Once he stopped . . ."), exhibits easily discernible elements of the biblical genre pattern. The person who gives the call "is going by"; that is, the shop is not the king's original goal. The person called is engaged in his humble profession, his name is given (though by the king, not the narrator), and the call removes him from his previous environment. A new life begins for him.

Setting in the Church and Redactional Setting

Ultimately, genre criticism tries to determine the setting of a genre in the life of the community. In other words, the attempt to group similar texts is not prompted simply by a love of classification, but by the desire to identify the social situation characterizing a particular genre pattern, the recurring situation in the life of a community where certain literary forms, those belonging to a particular genre, were used.

This is particularly true of oral tradition, since at the oral stage the transmission of various units of tradition is totally dependent on the social situations in which these units are regularly used. This is not true to the same extent once traditions have been committed to writing. Traditions that have come into writing can be lost or forgotten, but that they have been fixed in written form gives them a stronger tendency to persist than oral traditions.

The written form and the context in which it appears (a Gospel, for instance) limit the variations that a tradition can undergo. The literary context now accompanying a story such as that of Levi's call determines it semantically; that is, it fixes its meaning: Discipleship to Jesus is in this context to follow the gracious call of a Jesus who has come precisely to call sinners into his fellowship of forgiveness. The redactor's interpretation is not false, but it is, in fact, a redactional and spiritualizing interpretation of what was originally much more comprehensive. "Discipleship" was originally to "follow behind Jesus," and it encompassed everything implied by this fellowship of life and destiny.

This original meaning of the call stories can be more easily reconstructed from Mark's two other call stories (1:16-20). Mark places them at the beginning of his Gospel, which is in keeping with the fact that the element of new beginning is part of the original setting of the call story genre. The call prompts a person to give up an old existence and begin a new one. The old manner of existence is usually briefly evoked by the call coming while the one called is engaged in his daily professional life. This break with the past brought about by discipleship is usually portrayed by reference to the accoutrements of the person's professional world and to individuals from that person's social milieu. By choosing discipleship the person leaves all this behind for the sake of new and presumably higher values and more important personal relationships. This causes a break with natural or acquired relationships.

71

It is not surprising that a movement such as that surrounding Jesus, one so strongly characterized by the element of the newness of the inbreaking kingdom of God, should make such extensive use of the call story genre. It is also not surprising that this movement was able to enrich this genre with new content, as we have seen, and thus contribute to its development.

CHAPTER 7

Jesus' Disciples Pick Grain on the Sabbath (Mark 2:23-28; Matt 12:1-8)

Here again we are dealing with a passage in the threefold tradition, and the primary witness is Mark. Therefore, we will discuss the Markan version first. We will compare Matthew's version, which from a redaction-critical perspective has the most to offer, and will mention Luke only in passing.

Mark indicates the beginning of the text by the narrative signal "and it happened," by a temporal indicator ("on the sabbath"), and by a change of location ("through the grainfields"). Another change of location signals the end of the text after v. 28: "Again he entered the synagogue" (3:1).

Matthew marks the beginning of the text even more strongly. His version keeps the indications of time and location, but it also begins with a signal for the opening of a text: "At that time . . ." and mentions Jesus by name. This enhances the section's relative independence, while Mark presupposes that the reader already knows the name of the primary character from the previous context. Matthew also emphasizes more strongly the separation of this section from what follows. The change of location in Matt 12:9, which fixes the end of our text at v. 8, mentions not only the goal but also the point of departure for the movement: "And he went on from there. . . ."

THE FORM OF THE TEXT

Mark's text is clearly divided into two sections: A narrative introduction reporting the activity of Jesus and his disciples (v. 23) is followed by a

73

Mark 2:23-28	Matt 12:1-8

23a And it happened
  b that one sabbath he was going through the grainfields;
  c and his disciples,
  d as they made their way,
  e began to pluck ears of grain.
	1a At that time Jesus went through the grainfields on the sabbath;
	
	  b his disciples were hungry,
	  c and they began
	  d to pluck ears of grain
	  e and to eat.

24a And the Pharisees said to him,
 	
  b "Look,
  c why are they doing
  d what is not lawful on the sabbath?"
	2a But when the Pharisees saw it,
	  b they said to him,
	  c "Look,
	  d your disciples are doing
	  e what is not lawful to do on the sabbath."

25a And he said to them,
  b "Have you never read
  c what David did,
  d when he was in need
  e and was hungry, he and those who were with him:
26a how he entered the house of God,
  b when Abiathar was high priest,
  c and ate the bread of the Presence,
  d which it is not lawful for any but the priests to eat,
  e and gave it to those who were with him?"
	3a He said to them,
	  b "Have you not read
	  c what David did,
	
	  d when he was hungry, and those who were with him:
	4a how he entered the house of God
	
	  b and ate the bread of Presence,
	  c which was not lawful for him to eat nor for those who were with him, but only for the priests?

	5a Or have you not read in the law
	  b how on the sabbath the priests in the temple profane the sabbath
	  c and are guiltless?
	6a I tell you,
	  b something greater than the temple is here.

	7a And if you had known
	  b what this means,
	  c 'I desire mercy and not sacrifice,'
	  d you would not have condemned the guiltless.

27a And he said to them,
  b "The sabbath was made for
    humankind,
  c not humankind for the sabbath;	

28 therefore, the Son of man is Lord
    also of the sabbath."
	8 For the Son of man is Lord of
	   the sabbath."

dialogue between the Pharisees and Jesus (vv. 24-28). A renewed discourse introduction, "and he said to them" (v. 27a), divides Jesus' response to the Pharisees' question into an example from Scripture (vv. 25-26) and the conclusion (vv. 27-28), which is itself divided by "therefore" at the beginning of v. 28. This gives us the following structure:

Narrative introduction (v. 23)		
The opponents take offense (v. 24)		
Jesus' response (vv. 25-28)	The example of David (vv. 25-26)	
	The sabbath question (vv. 27-28)	v. 27
		v. 28

Tensions in the Text

At first, this text appears to be coherent: The Pharisees question Jesus because they consider his disciples' actions to be forbidden on the sabbath. Jesus' response refers to the example of David, who in a situation of need with his own followers also did what was forbidden. V. 27 elevates humankind above the sabbath and thus seems to follow the thematic thread introduced by the example of David, namely, that need knows no commandments. V. 28 can also be understood from the perspective of David's example: Just as David went beyond regulations, all the more Jesus, the Son of man, has the authority to do so, and as Lord of the sabbath he can sanction his disciples' actions just as David gave the bread of the presence to those who were with him and were hungry.

But closer observation discovers tensions that cast doubt on the text's original unity. First, Mark's narrative introduction does not make clear why the disciples were picking grain. Only in the light of the example from David's experience does it appear that they did so because they were hungry. Indeed, this is how the Matthean redactor understood

75

the text. He added that the disciples were hungry and that they ate the grain (Matt 12:1b, e). In so doing, he provides a closer connection between the narrative introduction and the example of David.

We then notice that the example of David does not mention the sabbath. What connects this example with the narrative introduction is only the doing of what is forbidden.[1] Furthermore, it is said that David himself, by giving his companions something to eat, did what was forbidden, while Jesus becomes involved only when the Pharisees address him — and they inquire only about the actions of his disciples, not about anything Jesus himself might have done.

The second part of Jesus' response is introduced by a renewed discourse introduction in the past tense (v. 27), as is the introduction to the Pharisees' question (v. 24a), while the earlier introduction of Jesus' words (v. 25) is in the present tense (literally "And he says"; use of the present tense in narratives of past events is common in the New Testament and is normally translated with the English past tenses).

Semantic problems arise in the connection of vv. 27 and 28. If we understand "therefore" in v. 28 as a conjunction signaling that a conclusion is being drawn, then Jesus' authority over the sabbath would have to be understood as a consequence of the creation of the sabbath for the sake of humankind. But then we would have to ask why this authority is not possessed by everyone or why the "Son of man" possesses some special authority over the sabbath. So v. 28 cannot be a conclusion drawn from v. 27. We can preserve the sense of the passage by putting a stronger break between the two verses and taking v. 28 as a summary of the entire text, that is, as the narrator's commentary rather than as a continuation of Jesus' words.

Finally, in v. 27 Jesus justifies his disciples' actions by pointing out that God gives us the sabbath. Thus the sabbath cannot obstruct what is useful to human beings. In contrast to this, the beginning and end of Jesus' response (vv. 24-26, 28) agree in placing the authority to sanction what is forbidden, that is, to suspend the sabbath, into the hands of one person. Although the principle that need knows no commandments

---

1. This is how Luke understands the Markan text. He inserts into the narrative introduction the statement that the disciples rubbed the grain in their hands (Luke 6:1). Grinding grain on the sabbath is forbidden. Luke thus finds it necessary, as does Matthew, to provide a closer connection between the narrative introduction and the example of David than does Mark. And like Matthew, Luke underscores this connection by inserting "and they ate."

plays a role in the example of David, it is nonetheless David himself who breaks the commandment for the sake of his companions. In this he resembles the "Son of man," who has authority over the sabbath and in this context also exercises that authority for the sake of his companions. In this way the beginning and end of Jesus' response are more closely related than either is to what comes between them.

TRADITION CRITICISM

We can begin in our attempt to deal with these tensions with the observation that the middle part of Jesus' response (v. 27) seems to be most closely related to the narrative introduction and to the Pharisees' question: The disciples do something on the sabbath that the Pharisees consider forbidden. V. 27 justifies this by pointing out that God created the sabbath for the sake of humankind.

Although the catchword "sabbath" also occurs in v. 28, the authority of the "Son of man" over the sabbath is not anticipated in any way in the narrative introduction. The introduction does not say that Jesus gave his disciples permission to pick grain on the sabbath. And the sabbath plays no role whatever in the example of David.

If we take the example of David (vv. 25-26) and the saying concerning the Son of man (v. 28) as later insertions, then the remaining text (vv. 23-24 + v. 27) is internally consistent. The discourse introduction in the past tense in v. 27 would no longer be in conflict with the present tense discourse introduction in v. 25, but would pick up the past tense of the discourse introduction in v. 24. Semantically, too, the text would now progress with no tensions and the difficulties that we have discovered would be eliminated.

GENRE CRITICISM

The story isolated from the Markan text by tradition criticism is a controversy dialogue. As expected in this genre, the text begins with a brief presentation of the setting (v. 23), followed by the opponents' objections in the form of a question (v. 24) and a short response by Jesus (v. 27).

The traditional unit we have isolated also points to a setting corresponding to that of the controversy dialogue genre. The background is found in the disputes of Hellenistic Jewish Christians with non-Christian Jews or, more likely, with conservative Jewish Christians. The story's liberal, even Gentile Christian, attitude toward the sabbath is justified in a way that remains within the realm of possibility within Jewish life, though it would be perceived as going beyond the practice of sabbath observance in some Jewish and Jewish Christian circles. In fact, this justification calls on Jewish traditions that place human beings and their needs over the sabbath. This justification is generally (and probably correctly) traced back to Jesus' own attitude toward the sabbath.

It is likely that the question of sabbath observance had already been solved by the time of the Markan redactor for the Christians he wrote for. This, then, could be taken as further evidence that the original form of the tradition is represented in vv. 23-24 + v. 27, since what is transmitted there would no longer have been of concrete relevance. The addition of vv. 25-26 and v. 28 alters not only the course of the argument, but also the text's function, giving it a relevance in the Markan situation.

REDACTION CRITICISM

Of these two additions, v. 28 most clearly betrays its redactional character, and does so initially with a single word: "the Son of man is Lord *also* of the sabbath." This small "also" places the text in a larger context, connecting it with the reference in v. 10 to the authority of "the Son of man" "to forgive sins." There Jesus' behavior, like that of his disciples here, causes his opponents to take offense, to which he responds, as he does here, with a claim to possess authority.

But the redactional theme of Jesus' authority comes up even earlier in Mark's Gospel. 1:22 refers to Jesus' authority in teaching, in 1:27 this teaching is called "new," and the miracle stories in 1:23-45 characterize this new teaching with authority as that which attracted great crowds. Similarly, the redactor believes that the behavior of Jesus' disciples on the sabbath reflects a "new" attitude. The offense taken by his opponents proves this. That Jesus' disciples do not fast like John's disciples and the Pharisees' disciples (2:18) is also considered "new," this "new" behavior corresponding to the "new" attitude and teaching that Jesus has inaugurated (2:19-22).

Mark 1:16-45 presents demonstrations of Jesus' authority before the people, and then 2:1–3:6 portrays Jesus' claim to authority as the Son of man before his opponents in five disputation scenes, 2:23-28 being the fourth of these scenes. Because of this claim to authority, Jesus' Galilean opponents decide to try to kill him (3:6). According to the Markan understanding, this claim to authority as the Son of man is, then, what ultimately leads to Jesus' condemnation by a Jewish court and his death on a Roman cross.

The expanded controversy dialogue in 2:23-28 thus loses the original function of the traditional unit and takes its place as one of five polemical scenes. The redactor does not argue for a view of the sabbath on the basis of creation theology, as did the original unit of tradition that he used as his source and as Jesus himself probably also did. He argues, instead, on the basis of christology: The disciples are permitted to break the sabbath because Jesus as the Son of man is Lord of the sabbath.

The example of David is also construed christologically. We have already seen that the references to David and to the Son of man (vv. 25-26, 28) resemble one another in that the disciples' forbidden action (breaking the sabbath) is justified in both cases by authorization from a superior. The example of David can accordingly be read christologically as a conclusion "from the lesser to the greater" (a favorite rabbinic device, often referred to in Latin as *a minore ad maius*): If David was able to give forbidden food to his companions to eat, all the more can Jesus permit his disciples to pick grain on the sabbath. As the "Son of man" he has authority over the sabbath and indeed has more authority than David himself. What our tradition-critical hypothesis judged negatively as an element not belonging to the original tradition, redaction criticism judges positively in view of its place in Markan christology.

FORM AND REDACTION CRITICISM OF MATTHEW'S VERSION

The common elements of the Matthean and Markan versions show that Matthew is dependent here on his Markan source, which he has altered redactionally. As we have seen, Matthew links the narrative introduction (Matt 12:1) more closely to the example of David by having the disciples pick grain because they are hungry and then having them eat it. He also puts more emphasis on the christological argument by totally ignoring the argument from creation theology (Mark 2:27). He simply omits Jesus' "dangerous" words. Furthermore, Matthew gives Mark's christological argumentation a characteristically Matthean accent by means of redactional additions (Matt 12:5-7).

Matthew divides Jesus' response into four parts and emphasizes this division with three formulaic introductions to Scripture references. Like Mark, he introduces the example of David with such a formula in the form of a question: "Have you not read . . . ?" (Matt 12:3). The same formula is repeated (v. 5), and the Scripture allusion thus introduced is connected with the example of David by a catchword, "priests," which has been added to the Markan source at the end of the sentence about David. The "priests" in the second Scripture reference are those who "profane the sabbath and are guiltless." They remain guiltless — this is the implication — because temple service, the priests' "sabbath work," has priority over the sabbath. The Matthean Jesus then draws a conclusion from the lesser to the greater: If the priests remain guiltless because of the temple, how much more does the disciples' fellowship with Jesus in the dawning messianic age permit them to break the sabbath. A catchword, "sabbath," allows Matthew to link this second Scripture reference to the narrative introduction.

The next Scripture is Hosea 6:6 (also used redactionally in Matt 9:13), introduced in a conditional clause that recalls the twofold question "have you not read?": "If you had known" or, perhaps, "If you had read" (Matt 12:7). Here again a catchword, "guiltless," provides a link back to the preceding argument (v. 5). To facilitate Jesus' accusation that his opponents have "condemned the guiltless," Matthew alters the Markan account by having the Pharisees address Jesus earlier not with a question, but with an assertion of the disciples' guilt (v. 2).

Matthew thus gives a threefold scriptural proof for his concluding statement: "For the Son of man is Lord of the sabbath." In characteristic Matthean fashion, the lordship of Jesus over the sabbath is proven at the very outset by Scripture itself, and indeed by Scripture in its entirety as law, writings, and prophets: The first proof (the example of David) is *haggadah*, that is, a narrative argument (the writings). The reference to the priests is a legal argument, or *halakah* (law). Finally, one of the prophets is quoted. For Matthew, the Jesus who alters sabbath observance is also the Messiah predicted by Scripture, the one who fulfills and completes the law and prophets (cf. 5:17).

80

CHAPTER 8

The Storm on the Sea I
(Mark 4:35-41)

Here again we have a text that comes to us in all three of the Synoptics. In accord with the two-source theory, we start from the assumption that Mark offers the primary text, while Matthew and Luke are dependent on Mark's version. We will begin with Mark and then turn to Matthew in the next chapter, since Matthew gives redaction criticism more to work with than Luke.

Mark identifies the beginning of this text with an indication of time in 4:35, which also provides a connection with the preceding material: "On that day, when evening had come." That the text has ended with v. 41 is signalled by a change of location in 5:1: "They came to the other side of the sea, to the country of the Gerasenes."

THE FORM OF THE TEXT

After a discourse introduction, the text begins with Jesus' command in direct address (v. 35). The disciples' execution of this command follows and involves a change in scene and characters (v. 36a-b). Because it involves another change of characters, we should take v. 36c separately: "And other boats were with him."

V. 37 also identifies itself as a new section by the introduction of a new character, so to speak, the storm. The action of this "character" proceeds from outside the boat toward the boat: "and the waves beat

Mark 4:35-41

35a	And he said to them on that day,
b	when evening had come,
c	"Let us go across to the other side."
36a	And leaving the crowd,
b	they took him with them, just as he was, in the boat.
c	And other boats were with him.
37a	And a great storm of wind arose,
b	and the waves beat against the boat,
c	so that the boat was already filling.
38a	But he was in the stern,
b	sleeping on the cushion.
c	And they woke him
d	and said to him,
e	"Teacher,
f	do you not care
g	if we perish?"
39a	And he awoke
b	and rebuked the wind,
c	and said to the sea,
d	"Peace!
e	Be still!"
f	And the wind ceased,
g	and there was a great calm.
40a	And he said to them,
b	"Why are you afraid?
c	Have you no faith?"
41a	And they were filled with awe,
b	and said to one another,
c	"Who is this,
d	that even wind and sea obey him?"

against the boat." The scene is set for the subsequent narrative by this description of the threatening situation.

In v. 38 the action takes place inside the boat. Jesus is sleeping in the boat's stern on the helmsman's cushion. In v. 38c-g the disciples turn to Jesus with a plea (in direct discourse) in the form of a question preceded by a vocative. Jesus then gives two imperatives to the wind and the sea (in direct discourse, v. 39d-e). V. 39f indicates a change both in "characters" and location: The storm and waves outside the boat become calm. V. 40 turns back to Jesus, who addresses the disciples with two questions. V. 41 then tells of the disciples' reaction.

This gives us the following segmentation of the text.

1. Jesus' order to cross over (v. 35)
2. the disciples' obedience (v. 36a-b)
3. the other boats (v. 36c)
4. storm and peril (v. 37)
5. Jesus asleep (v. 38a-b)
6. the disciples' plea (v. 38c-g)
7. Jesus' command to the storm (v. 39a-e)
8. the storm calmed (v. 39f-g)
9. Jesus' questions to the disciples (v. 40)
10. the disciples' reaction (v. 41)

Tensions in the Text

We can see clearly the connection between segments 1 and 2: Jesus' order prompts the disciples' obedience. The text underscores this with the remark "just as he was" to show that the disciples immediately and directly respond obediently to Jesus' command. So we can bracket these two segments together.

The relationship between segments 4 and 8 is similarly easy to discern. These two segments mark out the beginning and ending points of the narrative's action, that is, the movement from the activity of the storm to inactivity. The point of departure is carried over to the end point. As in any story, the beginning and end must be connected terminologically and by some sort of opposition so that the end does not constitute merely a cessation of the story: "The stages of the action are organized along the narrative axis. The narrative axis along which these stages are situated is generated by the contrast between the story's beginning and end. But in order to speak of a story's beginning and end, there must be some sort of conceptual opposition along the temporal axis. That is, the story is worth telling only if something in it has been altered."[1] Because of this relationship we can bracket segments 4-8 together.

Once this element of opposition becomes clear, we can see within segments 4-8 the relationship between segments 5 and 7, Jesus sleeping and then commanding the storm. The two segments are ordered sequentially along the narrative axis and are related by opposition: Jesus' inactivity becomes activity. We can also see that two pairs of segments, 4 and 5, which speak of the storm's activity and Jesus' inactivity, and 7 and 8, which speak of Jesus' activity and the storm's inactivity, are also related oppositionally. The initial opposition (4 and 5) has been reversed at the end (7 and 8).

The turning point or "peripeteia" of this narrative movement is segment 6. The disciples' plea (6) interprets Jesus' sleep (5) as unconcerned and powerless inactivity in the face of the storm (4). As such it motivates Jesus to command the wind and waves (7), and the great calm (8) comes about. From the perspective of the end we see that Jesus' sleep did not at all mean that he was unconcerned or helpless in the face of the storm. It points, rather, as Ambrose (fourth century) put it, to "the tranquility of his power."

The disciples, on the other hand, are seized with anxiety because of the storm's activity, and are driven to make their plea to Jesus. In contrast to Jesus' power, this plea reveals their helplessness in the face of the storm. This helplessness prompts Jesus to activate his power in an abrupt command to the wind and waves.

Segments 4-8 thus constitute a cohesive textual sequence within which the segments are structurally related; that is, they mutually interpret or semantically influence one another. Our search for tensions in the text will not find anything of interest here.

A more difficult question concerns the point of departure for segment 10, "the disciples' reaction." The disciples' question, "Who is this, that even wind and sea obey him?" can hardly be taken as an answer to Jesus' questions in segment 9, "Why are you afraid? Have you no faith?" Jesus' questions remain unanswered.

But his questions do look back to the disciples' plea (segment 6) and interpret it as an expression of fear and lack of faith. This reveals a previously unrecognized relationship between segments 5 and 6. We

---

1. K. H. Stierle, "Die Struktur narrativer Texte," *Funk-Kollege Literatur,* ed. H. Brackert and E. Lämmert (Frankfurt, 1977) I, 217. Sometimes the title itself of a work reveals this, as with *War and Peace* by L. Tolstoy.

have seen the contrast in actions between Jesus and his disciples as expressing the opposition between his tranquility and their anxiety in the face of the storm. And we took this to represent the contrast between "the tranquility of his power" and the disciples' agitation prompted by their helplessness in the face of natural forces.

But now we must notice that Jesus' questions in segment 9 interpret the disciples' plea in segment 6 as unbelief. If the disciples' agitation is lack of faith and is the opposite of Jesus' tranquility, then this tranquility must be an expression of Jesus' faith. Even though there is no direct connection between Jesus' questions in segment 9 and the disciples' reaction in segment 10, we must understand this reaction in the light of that question — as long as we take the text as it stands. Jesus' questions prompt us to interpret the disciples' question, "Who is this, that even wind and sea obey him?" as a further expression of their lack of faith and understanding: Not even Jesus' miraculous deed, the calming of the storm, is able to dispel their unbelief and open their eyes to him and his mystery. They still do not understand what it is that is reaching into their world in the person of Jesus. There is thus an important semantic relationship between segments 5, 6, 9, and 10.

But if segment 10 directly followed segment 8, the disciples' concluding question would be the appropriate reaction of those who have just witnessed a miraculous calming of a storm. The action would progress from an initial situation of distress to rescue from that distress to a concluding expression of fear and amazement. This would be quite characteristic of the genre. Segment 10 would be an echo of the overall

1. Jesus' order to cross over	v. 35	A
2. the disciples' obedience	v. 36a-b	
3. the other boats	v. 36c	
4. storm and peril	v. 37a-c	B
5. Jesus asleep	v. 38a-b	
6. the disciples' plea	v. 38c-g	
7. Jesus' command to the storm	v. 39a-e	
8. the storm calmed	v. 39f-g	
9. Jesus' questions to the disciples	v. 40	
10. the disciples' reaction	v. 41	C

action of the calming of the storm, underscoring in conclusion the miraculous nature of the events. Just as segments 1 and 2 provide the introduction to the narrative, so segment 10 would provide its conclusion.

In the text as it stands, however, segment 9 prevents this from being the case. Jesus' questions cause the concluding exclamation to be an expression of unbelief and misunderstanding that persists even after the miraculous events. Segment 9 also causes segments 5 and 6 to function on two semantic levels:

1. On the one hand, "Jesus' sleep" stands in contrast to the "disciples' plea" and shows "the tranquility of his power" in contrast to the anxiety of their powerlessness.
2. But in the light of Jesus' questions (segment 9), which take the disciples' plea as a sign of lack of faith, that very lack of faith is contrasted with Jesus' faith.

The result, then, is that the disciples occupy a more important role in the text. In segments 4-8 their plea is only the occasion for Jesus to command the storm to be calmed. Segment 9, however, causes the plea (as lack of faith) and the concluding reaction (as lack of understanding) to become themes in their own right.

Whereas segment 9, "Jesus' questions to the disciples," thus causes three other text elements to function semantically in two different ways, segment 3, the mention of the other boats accompanying Jesus, remains utterly without connection to any of the other segments. The other boats are never mentioned again, and the text would suffer no significant loss in meaning if one simply dropped segment 3.

So our examination of the text reveals that two text segments are connected either not at all or only weakly to the others. These inconsistencies in the text suggest that we ought to investigate it from the perspective of tradition and redaction criticism. We need to ask, that is, whether we can distinguish a pre-Markan form of the text from the Markan redaction that has resulted in the text's present form.

TRADITION CRITICISM

The other boats that "were with him" (segment 3), as we have seen, have nothing to do with anything else in the text. Their absence would change nothing. It is unlikely that mention of them is a redactional insertion into the older tradition, since the addition would serve no purpose. And it is a bit farfetched to think that the redactor considered the one boat mentioned in his source too small "to hold the twelve disciples and the others mentioned in 4:10" and so put additional means of transportation at their disposal.[2] It is more likely that we are dealing with a "splinter of tradition,"[3] that is, a part of the pre-Markan story that had a meaning that has been lost in the redactor's elimination or obscuring of other details in the story .

Segment 9, Jesus' questions to the disciples, also does not fit into the network of relationships among the other segments. Only against the background of this segment do we understand the disciples' fear and plea as a lack of understanding of what has happened, whereas without it their amazement would be the expected conclusion and reaction to the calming of the storm. So it is sensible to conclude that segment 9 was added to the traditional unit, perhaps as late as the redactional stage.

In addition to solving the ambiguities we have seen in segments 5, 6, and 10, identifying segment 9 as a later addition might also enable us to reintegrate segment 3 into the text. The people in the other boats would in that case be those who react in fear to the miraculous events — a traditional feature in biblical stories in which a divine event is

2. So J. Gnilka, *Das Evangelium nach Markus* (Einsiedeln/Neukirchen, 1978) 193; similarly R. H. Gundry, *Mark: A Commentary on His Apology for the Cross* (Grand Rapids: Eerdmans, 1993) 238.

3. R. Pesch, *Das Markusevangelium* (Freiburg/Basel/Vienna, 1976) I, 270: "the mention of other boats accompanying Jesus . . . which cannot be clarified with any certainty." Pesch lists other views, each of which seeks to distinguish the text as we have it from the traditional unit (one by a text-critical hypothesis):

1. The circle of witnesses to the miracle was originally larger, and has now been limited to the disciples (G. Schille). 2. An earlier stage of tradition may have intensified the threatening situation by telling how the "other boats" sank in the storm (G. Theissen). 3. The original reading was that "other boats" had *not* accompanied Jesus (E. Lohmeyer). 4. Perhaps the accompanying boats are to function as witnesses to the miraculous events (R. Schnackenburg; similarly also E. Schweizer).

Another view is that the "other boats," whether traditional or redactional, are mentioned to make the story a closer fulfillment of Psalm 107:23-30: D. E. Nineham, *Saint Mark* (Pelican New Testament Commentaries; New York: Penguin, 1963) 148; cf. C. Myers, *Binding the Strong Man: A Political Reading of Mark's Story of Jesus* (Maryknoll, NY: Orbis, 1988) 196.

witnessed. These people would then give the story its conclusion by crying out as a chorus, "Who is this, that even wind and sea obey him?"

But this prompts us to ask about the genre to which our reconstructed traditional unit belongs and about the redactor's intentions: What prompted him to insert Jesus' question (segment 9) into the tradition he had before him? That is, what is the new literary setting that this unit of tradition has acquired through its redactional inclusion in its present context? Only by answering this question can we secure the results of our tradition-critical work.

GENRE CRITICISM

Interpreters have traditionally categorized this story among those telling of miracles in the natural sphere, which they distinguish from stories of healing miracles and exorcisms. But we should disregard this designation since it is based on only one feature of the story and tends to bypass any understanding of the features of the genre to which this story belongs.

One can, however, grant that the story belongs to the genre of the miracle story, specifically that of the "story of miraculous rescue" with its characteristic thematic structure: "After the introductory scene (vv. 35-36), this genre describes the situation of distress (v. 37), the plea for help (v. 38b-c) with the motif of the 'withdrawal of the miracle worker,' the deliverance (exorcism) effected by the miracle-working word (v. 39a-b), the recognition of the miracle (v. 39c-d), admiration (v. 41a), and acclamation (v. 41b-c)."[4]

But there are features and motifs in the story that are not characteristic of a straightforward miracle story. That the genre of exorcism has had some influence is particularly apparent when Jesus commands the wind and sea to "be silent" (cf. Mark 1:25), particularly because this command prompts the reader to understand these natural phenomena almost as personified powers, "as living beings whose threatening animate gestures are beaten back by Jesus' words."[5]

4. R. Pesch, loc. cit., 268f. See also G. Theissen, *The Miracle Stories of the Early Christian Tradition*, trans. Francis McDonagh (Philadelphia: Fortress Press, 1983) 47ff.
5. K. Kertelge, *Die Wunder Jesu im Markusevangelium. Eine redaktionsgeschichtliche Untersuchung* (Munich, 1970) 92.

This personification of storm and sea can be traced back to concepts found in ancient creation myths, in which the primeval powers of chaos, often personified as a dragon or snake, are vanquished in battle with the deity. Genesis 1 reflects such myths, as do other parts of the Hebrew Bible, but does not speak of an actual battle between God and the powers of chaos. It "demythologizes" these powers by having God create and order the world simply by means of his creative word.

Jesus is portrayed in the story of the calming of the sea as having power over the chaotic forces of storm and sea. The story thus transcends the framework both of miracle stories as such and also of other stories of deliverance from maritime distress. It transfers to Jesus what is normally reserved for God alone, namely, the creative power of the word, and attributes to Jesus what is said in, for example, Psalm 89:10f. But one could speak this way about Jesus only after Easter. The narrative presupposes the insight of faith arising from the resurrection event, in which Jesus conquered death, the ultimate power of chaos.

The story allows the disciples to witness this event that reveals the creative word of God that Jesus speaks. It belongs, therefore, among stories that "narrate the miracles from the standpoint of epiphany," stories, that is, "in which the divine power of the divine wonder-worker becomes manifest."[6]

In portraying this epiphany, the story of the calming of the storm employs the topos of miraculous rescue. Already in the Hebrew Bible accounts of God's creative acts were not told simply for their own sake: Power to effect salvation and deliverance is attributed to these acts of epiphany. As in Psalm 65:7, so also in this story about Jesus, subjugation of the sea's chaotic power, which has threatened creation, parallels the subjugation of human enemies. Our search for the setting in which this epiphany story was used must, then, consider its background in the Hebrew Bible, since it arose in an environment thoroughly familiar with the ancient biblical world.

The transfer to Jesus of what in the Hebrew Bible is reserved for God alone, namely, the power of creation, represents a christology that understands Jesus as the epiphany of God. This is precisely what the epiphany story asserts. It has, therefore, a missionary function, exhorting its readers to believe in Jesus as the revelation of God the creator.

6. M. Dibelius, *From Tradition to Gospel*, trans. B. L. Woolf (New York: Scribner, n.d.) 150, 94.

We may well doubt whether this story accomplished its purpose with Jewish audiences. A pious Jew would perceive this transfer of God's creative power to a human being as blasphemy, even though the story's background is influenced by Hebrew thinking.

But the story might have arisen in an environment where there were both Jewish and Gentile Christians: The mission to the Gentiles also influenced the character of this epiphany story, which draws on concepts from the Hebrew Bible. The author might also have relied on knowledge of Hellenistic stories in which "deliverance from disaster at sea occurs primarily through the epiphany of a God who is summoned in prayer."[7] But in contrast to these Gentile epiphany stories, this story about Jesus does not tell of an epiphany of a God who disappears again after he reveals himself. It tells rather of the epiphany of God's creative power in the commanding words of Jesus, who is with the disciples in the boat at both the beginning and the end of the story. Furthermore, it does not tell of the actions of a God responsible for a specific sphere (sea journeys, for instance), but rather of the creator God himself revealed in Jesus' words, a God who is able to control chaos both authoritatively and comprehensively.

This work of genre criticism has confirmed our tradition-critical hypothesis: The textual unit established by tradition criticism can be identified as belonging to an independent genre.

REDACTION CRITICISM

In its quest for the intentions of the redactor, redaction criticism focuses on many of the same features that genre criticism investigates, at least in those instances where redactional alterations have affected both the text's function and its genre. If v. 40 is, in fact, a redactional insertion, we must be able to show that Jesus' questions there reveal the redactor's intentions and that those same intentions are discernible in other parts of the text as a whole, that is, in the Gospel of Mark, that can justifiably be identified as redactional. And in fact the theme of the disciples' unbelief and misunderstanding occurs frequently in

7. R. Pesch, *Markusevangelium* I, 274; cf. Pesch's examples.

other parts of Mark's Gospel, as can be seen with the help of a concordance.[8]

While the motif of the disciples' lack of faith and understanding
can clearly be shown to be a theme of the Markan redaction, the idea
of Jesus' "faith" in the story of the calming of the storm is more problematic. And yet, it, too, occurs redactionally elsewhere in Mark, and
does so in connection with the motif of the disciples' unbelief and
incomprehension. In the story of the healing of an epileptic boy, the
disciples are unable to heal the boy because they belong to the "faithless
generation" that Jesus is unable to bear any longer (9:19). On the other
hand, Jesus' ability to bring about the healing is attributed to his faith,

---

8. In Mark Jesus' opponents decide against him from the beginning and are
determined to seek his death (3:6). Though the people come to him in droves at the
beginning, they are nonetheless "obdurate"; indeed, his teaching itself drives them into
their obduracy (4:11). They "see and yet do not see." But the disciples, in contrast, "are
always with him." Though the people surround Jesus wherever he goes (1:33, 37, 45;
2:1f.; 3:7-9, 20; 4:1; 5:21, 31; 6:31, 33f., 55; 8:1), they are not around him continually,
and their numbers begin to dwindle soon after the first prediction of the Passion (8:31).

> But the disciples are called and come to him as those whom he himself wanted.
> He created them (3:14) so that they would be with him. Again and again they
> are alone with him, in his house, by themselves; they are there, and he teaches
> them (cf. 7:17-23). Though their own obduracy prevents the disciples from
> understanding Jesus' words and deeds, their perseverance in his presence does
> allow them to remember misunderstood details. Because they have remained
> with him, they are able to respond to his question concerning the number of
> baskets (8:19). What they do not understand is the hidden meaning. They are
> unable to put the details into any sort of order because their blindness conceals
> the mystery, and their deafness fails to hear the summons. (F. Schnider and
> W. Stenger, *Johannes und die Synoptiker. Vergleich ihrer Parallelen* [Munich, 1971]
> 122f.)

The disciples' lack of understanding continues to the cross and reaches a climax
with Peter's denial and the disciples' escape. Though they follow Jesus to Jerusalem, they
abandon him after his arrest. They are obdurate, uncomprehending, and ultimately
unbelieving. What is particularly incomprehensible to them is the necessity of suffering
(e.g., 8:32).

Their blindness to God's activity revealed in Jesus means that the epiphanies (the
calming of the storm, the transfiguration) remain misunderstood. Ultimately, only Jesus'
resurrection can eliminate their misunderstanding and make faith possible. This motif
of the disciples' incomprehension is for Mark a "diatribe against the unbelief of the
community" (E. Wendling, *Die Entstehung des Marcus-Evangeliums* [Tübingen, 1908]
73f., cited by Pesch, loc. cit.), though also a reference to the necessity of God's act in
Jesus' resurrection, which alone gives to the disciples' access to the "secret of the kingdom
of God" (4:11) present in Jesus.

for "all things are possible to him who believes" (9:23). This formula, "all things are possible," refers in Mark (10:27; 14:36) and in the biblical tradition as a whole[9] to God's omnipotence, which is grounded in his creative power. Therefore, the person who believes — and here that means Jesus himself — participates in God's omnipotence.

This should adequately establish that Jesus' questions in Mark 4:40 are a product of the Markan redaction. This verse introduces into the story of the calming of the storm the themes of the disciples' lack of faith and of Jesus' faith. It also directs the reader's attention more strongly toward the disciples. In the original traditional unit the disciples, through their anxious plea, function merely to prompt Jesus to reveal his power. After the calming of the storm their choral conclusion serves to throw into relief once more that dimension of the epiphany event which transcends the earthly sphere. But now, in the redactionally reworked version, the function of the disciples in the story follows a specific line of Markan theology, as we have seen.

This recognition of Mark's focus on the disciples' incomprehension is important not only because it is part of a theme recurring throughout the Gospel but also because by inserting Jesus' questions in the story Mark reflects and theologically deepens the epiphany christology of his source. The traditional unit equipped Jesus with God's own creative power and spoke of him in a way that the Bible normally reserves for God. Mark preserves this christology and deepens it by indicating indirectly, through the contrasting example of the disciples' unbelief, that Jesus' own faith is the ground of God's creative power, which Jesus both represents and exercises. This creative power is thus based on faith, and in Mark this faith is the relationship with God that only Jesus has.

After the story of the calming of the sea Mark's Gospel places two miracle stories, which both also present striking examples of the miraculous: an exorcism of two thousand spirits and the raising of a dead person. Before these three stories we have what is known as the "parable chapter" (4:1-33); there Mark presents examples of Jesus' teaching. Similarly, at the beginning of his Gospel Mark characterizes Jesus' teaching as that of one who has "authority" and follows the remark that Jesus "taught" (1:21) with an exorcism (1:23-26) and a miraculous

9. Ecclesiastes 8:3; Wisdom 12:18 (cf. 11:23); Job 10:13; 42:2 — all passages from the wisdom literature! Cf. also Psalm 115:3.

healing (1:29-31). We can thus assume that it is no accident that the first extensive and ordered presentation of Jesus' teaching (4:1-33) is followed by three stories showing how God's creative power is revealed in Jesus' acts as that which conquers chaos, spirits, and death. Since these stories speak of God's creative power revealing itself in Jesus' acts of power, Jesus' "teaching with authority" also acquires the status of God's word itself.

CHAPTER 9

The Storm on the Sea II
(Matt 8:18-27)

The story of the calming of the storm also occurs in Matthew and Luke (8:22-25), both of whom, we can assume, used Mark as their source for the story. But both also altered their source and placed the story in different contexts. Since the "tradition" available to Matthew in this story was thus the Markan version of the story, our focus can be on Matthew's handling of the Markan story, that is, on redaction criticism. But form criticism also comes into the picture, since the Matthean redactional alterations affect the structure of the text.

Matt 8:18 sets the scene for the story and echoes Mark 4:35. But in vv. 19-23 Matthew has inserted additional material into his Markan source, material that occurs in Luke in a different place (Luke 9:57-62) and in a slightly different form. Matthew drew this material from his second source, Q, which was also available to Luke. The inserted material, Jesus' two-part dialogue with a scribe (Matt 8:19-20) and with a disciple (vv. 21-22), should be taken as part of Matthew's version of the story of the calming of the storm.

THE FORM OF THE TEXT

Jesus' order to cross over to the other shore (v. 18) is, then, not immediately followed by its execution in Matthew. The first part of the inserted dialogue begins when a scribe approaches Jesus and declares his readiness for discipleship (v. 19). The second begins when a disciple

94

Mark 4:35-41   Matt 8:18-27

	Mark			Matt	
35	Jesus' order to cross over		18	Jesus' order	
36a-b	The disciples' obedience ←				
36c	The other boats				
			19 20	I a) Declaration of discipleship b) Warning against hasty acceptance of discipleship	
			21 22	II a) Qualified readiness for discipleship b) Exhortation for complete discipleship	
			→ 23	The disciples' obedience: discipleship	
37	Storm and peril		24a	Quaking and peril	
38a-b	Jesus asleep		24b	Jesus asleep	
38c-g	The disciples' plea		25	The disciples' plea	
39a-e	Jesus' command to the storm ←				
			→ 26a	Jesus' question to the disciples	
			→ 26b	Jesus' command to the storm	
39f-g	The storm calmed		26c	The storm calmed	
40	Jesus' questions to the disciples ←				
41	The disciples' reaction		27	Choral conclusion	

addresses Jesus and asks for postponement (v. 21). These two characters are contrasted with each other by their identifications, scribe vs. "another of his disciples," and by what they say: The scribe calls Jesus "teacher," the disciple calls him "Lord"; the one who is already a disciple limits his willingness to act as a disciple by asking for postponement, while the scribe, who is not yet a follower of Jesus, declares his readiness to be one. Jesus' responses (vv. 20 and 22) correspond similarly. He warns the scribe against a hasty decision for discipleship. But he calls the disciple to unconditional and unqualified discipleship. Only then does Matthew have the disciples get into the boat. The order to cross over and the execution of the order thus frame the two-part dialogue.

From that point, Matthew's narrative sequence follows the Markan source through the storm's peril, Jesus asleep, and the disciples' plea. But then Jesus' question to the disciples immediately follows the disciples' plea, whereas in Mark the questions occur only after the storm has been calmed. Matthew thus avoids what has happened in Mark, namely, Jesus' words interpreting the disciples' plea only through a long reference back to them.

The command to the storm is no longer in direct discourse in Matthew. As in Mark, though, the storm is immediately calmed. Because Matthew has placed Jesus' question to the disciples before the calming of the storm, he is able to use the reaction of "the people" as a choral conclusion directly after the miracle and to separate it from Jesus' reprimanding words, which in Mark causes the reaction — there attributed to the disciples — to be interpreted as incomprehension. But this has already brought us into the sphere of redaction criticism, which uses a more precise comparison to see if Matthew's alterations of his Markan source say anything about his particular intentions.

REDACTION CRITICISM

Mark gave the disciples a greater role in this story than they had in the tradition handed down to him. He did so by drawing attention to their unbelief and incomprehension. In Matthew's version the disciples are similarly more important for the story, though the redactional intentions are different from those of Mark. The insertion of the two-part dialogue (vv. 19-22) introduces the theme of discipleship, of following Jesus, which connects the two parts of the dialogue: The prospective disciple is warned; the disciple asking for postponement is exhorted to unhesitating fulfillment. This lends to the calming of the storm, which follows, a thematic focus before it even begins: The story is to show what discipleship really means.

This immediately affects the story's beginning: In Mark the disciples take Jesus into the boat, but in Matthew he precedes them, and the disciples "follow after" him; here already Matthew picks up the thematic catchword of the inserted dialogue (v. 23). Though most translations obscure this point, Matthew does not speak of a "storm," but rather of a "shaking" or "quaking" (Greek *seismos*). Furthermore, the waves are already swamping the boat, not merely threatening it as in

Mark. Matthew underscores the significance of all this with "and behold!" at the beginning of v. 24. He also amplifies the contrast between the storm and Jesus' sleep by omitting the elements Mark uses to describe Jesus' sleep (the stern, the helmsman's cushion).

A concordance can enlighten us concerning Matthew's redactional intentions, since he speaks redactionally of "quaking" in three other passages in his Gospel, twice introducing it with "and behold!":

- At Jesus' death the earth "quakes," rocks are split, and the bodies of deceased saints rise from their tombs and appear in the city (27:51-53).
- An earthquake occurs when the women go to Jesus' tomb, and then the angel of the Lord descends from heaven and rolls back the stone. Those guarding the tomb are seized by these events, "quake," and become like dead men (28:1-4).
- When Jesus enters Jerusalem, the whole city "quakes" and asks, "Who is this?" (21:20).

In two of these passages Matthew employs the biblical theophany motif — when God appears, the earth quakes — in connection with the idea of a resurrection of the dead. But the resurrection is an eschatological event. According to Matthew, then, Jesus' crucifixion and resurrection are part of the events of the end time.

Accordingly, we may assume that Matthew changes Mark's "storm" into a "quaking" because he understands the situation of the disciples' peril in the boat as an eschatological event. Although their discipleship does bring them together with Jesus, it also brings them into the final tribulations and distress, during which Jesus sleeps. At least this is how it appears for the disciples.

Not surprisingly, Matthew also alters the disciples' anxious plea into a prayer-like petition: With the address "Lord" the disciples turn to Jesus as the one who has been taken up to the Father, the one who remains invisible to his church, but who as the exalted one is also with the church "to the close of the age" (28:20). And in Matthew the plea is followed immediately by Jesus' words to the disciples.

But Matthew has eliminated from the story the motif of the disciples' incomprehension and unbelief. The disciples are not merely those who lack understanding of Jesus. Their relationship with him is characterized rather by the contrast between the knowledge in their confession of faith and the smallness of their faith, in which they see only their distress — rather than the person who is with them.

In Matthew the disciples prefigure the church. Though the church knows of the Lord's presence (28:20), it is nonetheless repeatedly threatened by weakness of faith (6:30; 8:26; 14:31; 16:8; 17:20). This weakness is not unbelief, as in Mark, but faith that is simply too weak, "that is paralyzed in the storm (8:26; 14:31) and in anxiety (6:30; 16:8), and thus is exposed as an appearance of faith (17:20), which is not sufficiently mature to withstand the pressure of demonic powers,"[1] particularly not that of the eschatological tribulations through which the church must go.

Matthew's conclusion confirms that he sees in these disciples "of little faith" the church itself in its discipleship; again altering Mark, he attributes the amazed choral conclusion (v. 41) to "the people," without having said anything previously about anyone having accompanied Jesus and the disciples. It is the continuing event of the deliverance of the church itself from eschatological tribulation that prompts outsiders to be seized by wonder.

Matthew has placed the Markan motif of Jesus' teaching with authority (Mark 1:22, 27: "not as the scribes") at the end of the Sermon on the Mount (Matt 7:28f.), which presents Jesus in his initial programmatic discourse as the Messiah who completes the Torah and announces the coming of the "greater righteousness" (17:20), that is, as the Messiah of the word. This first discourse is followed by several miraculous deeds in chapters 8–9, which have been assembled from Mark and Q (8:5-13) or redactionally composed (9:27-33). After presenting Jesus as the Messiah of the word, Matthew thus characterizes Jesus as the Messiah of the deed.

The calming of the storm is in the middle of this section focusing on deeds and is followed, as in Mark, by an exorcism on the other side of the sea. The two stories together characterize Jesus as the one acting with God's authority, so that, as anyone can see, "the blind receive their sight, the lame walk, lepers are cleansed, the deaf hear, and the dead are raised up" (11:4-5), just as the messianic teaching, that is, "good news preached to the poor" (11:5), has been heard in the Sermon on the Mount. Both teaching and deeds qualify Jesus as the one "who is to come" (11:3).

---

1. G. Bornkamm, "The Stilling of the Storm in Matthew," *Tradition and Interpretation in Matthew*, by G. Bornkamm, G. Barth, and H. J. Held, trans. P. Scott (Philadelphia: Westminster, 1963) 52.

CHAPTER 10

The Centurion of Capernaum
(Matt 8:5-13; Luke 7:1-10)

The healing of a servant or son of a Gentile centurion or royal official is recounted in Matthew, Luke, and John. The Matthean and Lukan versions are close enough that we may assume that they are based on the same source, that is, on Q. The Johannine version (John 4:46-54), on the other hand, is quite different from the Synoptic version, although the same substance underlies it. We will assume that the Gospel of John was not written in direct literary dependence on the Synoptics,[1] and on this basis will examine the Matthean and Lukan versions of the story before turning to the Johannine story in the next chapter. Because of their basis in Q, our work on the Matthean and Lukan story will be focused on source criticism and redaction criticism.

Changes of place and of characters mark Matt 8:5 as the text's beginning and v. 13 as its conclusion. In the Matthean version, a healing from leprosy (taken over from Mark 1:40-45) precedes the healing of the centurion's servant at the foot of the mountain immediately after the Sermon on the Mount (Matt 8:1). In 8:5 Jesus enters Capernaum, and the Gentile centurion approaches him as a supplicant. In v. 14 Jesus enters Peter's house, where he heals Peter's mother-in-law (cf. Mark 1:29-34).

In Luke the story begins in 7:1, immediately after the end of the Sermon on the Plain (which corresponds to Matthew's Sermon on the Mount). In v. 11 an indication of time and change of place signal the

---

1. See the discussion in R. E. Brown, *The Gospel according to John* (Anchor Bible; Garden City, NY: Doubleday, 1966) I, xliv-xlvii.

Matthew 8:5-13   Luke 7:1-10

		1a	After he had ended all his sayings in the hearing of the people
5a	As he entered Capernaum		
		b	he entered Capernaum.
b	a centurion came to him	2a	A centurion had a slave
c	beseeching him	b	who was sick
d	and saying:	c	and at the point of death.
6a	"Lord,	d	He was dear to him.
b	my servant *(pais)* is lying paralyzed at home,	3a	When he heard of Jesus
c	in terrible distress."	b	he sent to him elders of the Jews,
		c	asking him
		d	to come
		e	and heal his slave.
		4a	And when they came to Jesus,
		b	they besought him earnestly,
		c	saying,
		d	"He is worthy
		e	to have you do this for him,
		5a	for he loves our nation,
		b	and he built us our synagogue."
7a	And he said to him,	6a	And Jesus went with them.
b	"I will come and heal him."		
		b	When he was not far from the house,
8a	But the centurion answered him,	c	the centurion sent friends to him,
		d	saying to him,
b	"Lord,	e	"Lord,
		f	do not trouble yourself,
c	I am not worthy	g	for I am not worthy
d	to have you come under my roof;	h	to have you come under my roof;
		7a	therefore I did not consider myself worthy
		b	to come to you.
e	but only say the word,	c	But say the word,
f	and my servant will be healed.	d	and my servant is healed.

9a	For I am a man under authority,	8a	For I am a man under authority,
b	with soldiers under me;	b	with soldiers under me:
c	and I say to one,	c	and I say to one,
d	'Go,'	d	'Go,'
e	and he goes,	e	and he goes;
f	and to another,	f	and to another,
g	'Come,'	g	'Come,'
h	and he comes,	h	and he comes;
i	and to my slave,	i	and to my slave,
j	'Do this,'	j	'Do this,'
k	and he does it."	k	and he does it."
10a	When Jesus heard him,	9a	When Jesus heard this
b	he marveled,	b	he marveled at him,
		c	and turned
c	and said to those who followed him,	d	and said to the multitude that followed him,
d	"Truly,		
e	I say to you,	e	"I tell you,
f	with no one in Israel have I found such faith.	f	not even in Israel have I found such faith."
			13:28-29
11a	I tell you,	28	*There you will weep and gnash your teeth, when you see Abraham and Isaac and Jacob and all the prophets in the kingdom of God and you yourselves thrust out.*
b	many will come from east and west		
c	and sit at table with Abraham, Isaac, and Jacob in the kingdom of heaven,		
12	while the sons of the kingdom will be thrown into outer darkness."	29	*And people will come from east and west and from north and south and sit at table in the kingdom of God.*
13a	And Jesus said to the centurion,		
b	"Go.		
c	As you have believed,		
d	so be it done to you."		
e	And the servant was healed at that very hour.	10a	And when those who had been sent returned to the house,
		b	they found the slave well.

beginning of the story of the young man of Nain, which Luke acquired from a source to which he alone had access (often referred as "L").

THE FORM OF THE TEXTS

Since the text in Matt 8:5-13 consists almost completely of direct discourse, its segmentation is signaled by changes in speaker:

1. Encounter with the miracle worker and petition for healing (vv. 5-6)
2. Declaration of willingness (v. 7)
3. Modified petition for healing, with justification (vv. 8-9)
4. Jesus words to his companions (vv. 10-12)
5. Jesus' healing words to the centurion (v. 13a-d)
6. The healing (v. 13e)

Luke's text is somewhat more complicated because it includes additional characters and alternates between direct and indirect discourse. Nonetheless, its segmentation is still fairly straightforward:

1. Connection to preceding text and Jesus' change of location (v. 1)
2. Description of the situation (v. 2)
3. The first group of emissaries sent with the petition for healing (indirect discourse), its justification (direct discourse) (vv. 3-5)
4. Jesus' departure with the emissaries (v. 6a)
5. The second group of emissaries sent with the modified petition (vv. 6b-8)
6. Jesus words to the multitude (v. 9)
7. Return of the emissaries and recognition of the healing (v. 10)

COMPARISON OF THE TWO VERSIONS

Among the more important differences, Matthew does not include either of the two groups of emissaries (Luke 7:3-8, 10), which is, then, either a Matthean deletion or a Lukan redactional addition. In connection with this, the petition for healing on the lips of the centurion occurs only in Matthew (Matt 8:6) and the centurion's remark, "Therefore I did not presume to come to you," occurs only in Luke (Luke 7:7).

Furthermore, Matt 8:11-12 does not occur in this story in Luke, who includes these verses in a different context (13:28-29). But the agreements in this material show that it does come from Q. Either Matthew inserted the verses here, or Luke deleted them from the story and put them elsewhere.

There are also less significant differences. It is not entirely clear whether Matthew is referring to the centurion's "servant" or "child" since the Greek word *pais* allows either translation. Luke clearly refers to the centurion's "servant" or "slave" (Greek *doulos*). The symptoms of the illness are portrayed differently: In Matthew the sick person is "paralyzed" and "in terrible distress" (Matt 8:6). In Luke he is "at the point of death" (Luke 7:2). The remark that the slave "was dear" to the centurion (Luke 7:2) does not occur in Matthew. Jesus' words of healing (Matt 8:13) do not occur in Luke. Instead, the returning emissaries are involved in the confirmation of success (Luke 7:10). Matthew mentions the "very moment" of healing (cf. John 4:52f.).

Source and Redaction Criticism

The version of the story in the source used by Matthew and Luke emerges only when we specify exactly what redactional alterations have been made by both Gospel writers.

Linguistic observations supported by a concordance point to some Matthean redactional changes: "Kingdom of heaven" (Matt 8:11), for example (Luke 13:28 speaks instead of the "kingdom of God"), is one of Matthew's favorite phrases. Furthermore, only Matthew speaks of "sons of the kingdom" (Matt 8:12; 13:38) and of "outer darkness" (Matt 8:12; 22:13; 25:30).

The evidence concerning the saying in Matt 8:11 is more complicated. Matthew changes the saying from second person plural, which is the form of the saying in Luke 13:28, to third person plural. This removes the saying from a situation of direct address and changes it into an eschatological promise for Gentiles and a prediction of disaster for Jews. The Matthean form of the saying thus underscores and elaborates on the idea expressed in Matt 8:10, which speaks of the centurion's exemplary faith, found in no Israelite. Vv. 11f. thus continue the topic of the difference between Jews and Gentiles.

Matthew's community consisted of both Jewish and Gentile Christians who were still under considerable Jewish influence and in competition with a purely Jewish community. From Matthew's experience in this community it became clear that Gentiles were open to the Christian proclamation. As the "new Israel" they were receiving the promise of eschatological table fellowship with Israel's ancestors. In contrast, the majority of Jews closed themselves off from the Christian proclamation. From Matthew's perspective this excluded them from the eschatological gift of the kingdom of heaven, although they as "sons of the kingdom" should have been its legitimate heirs. Thus we may assume that Matt 8:11-12, which originally came from Q, was inserted redactionally by Matthew into the story of the centurion.

In Luke this story is followed by the story of the raising from the dead of the young man of Nain. Perhaps Luke has amplified the symptoms of the illness from "paralyzed" (Matt 8:6) to mortal danger (Luke 7:2), thus tracing a movement from one story to the next and anticipating Jesus' response to John's inquiry: "The dead are raised" (v. 22).

We must take a closer form-critical look at the motif of the emissaries in order to determine whether it was traditional and omitted by Matthew or added redactionally by Luke. In both versions of the story it is significant that a religious antithesis exists between Jesus and the centurion. That Jesus is a Jew and the centurion a Gentile provides one of the essential features to the action: It is at the behest of a Gentile that Jesus does not enter a Gentile house! Luke underscores this antithesis through the motif of the two groups of emissaries. The Gentile centurion first sends as emissaries those who are more closely associated with Jesus the Jew, namely, the "elders of the Jews." When Jesus gets closer to the house, the centurion then sends persons who are more closely associated with himself, namely, his "friends." The distance between Jesus and the centurion is thus made to seem even greater: Two sets of mediators are required to bridge the gulf.

The first emissaries themselves judge the centurion to be "worthy" (Luke 7:4), but the later emissaries quote the centurion himself: "I did not consider myself worthy to come to you." This use of the same word focuses the contrast between appraisal of the centurion by others and his self-appraisal. His self-appraisal thus becomes an example of humility. That he sends emissaries also serves this purpose, since he does not presume to come to Jesus himself.

In Matthew's version the centurion does come to Jesus, but he does not allow Jesus to enter his house; his justification is that "I am not worthy to have you come under my roof" (Matt 8:8). Here, too, the centurion exhibits humility, but this humility functions only to anticipate Jesus' statement about faith (v. 10). Though the statement about faith also occurs in Luke (Luke 7:9), that Jesus does not, in fact, enter the centurion's house is amplified in Luke: Only the emissaries, not the centurion himself, actually meet Jesus. This, with the contrast between the centurion's self-appraisal and his appraisal by others, focuses the Lukan story on the centurion's "virtues": His humility is presented alongside his faith.

This Lukan focus on the centurion's "virtues" is also reinforced by the statement made by the Jewish elders: They characterize the centurion as a "God fearer," that is, as a Gentile who is attracted by the Jewish understanding of God and by Jewish ethical thinking but who has not taken the final step of becoming a "proselyte," a circumcised Gentile convert to Judaism obligated to keep the whole Mosaic law. Furthermore, he has acted out his sympathy toward Judaism in an act of generosity: "He built our synagogue." Luke's remark that the slave "was dear to him" follows along these same lines. Although antiquity certainly attests examples of personal friendship between masters and slaves, such relationships were exceptional. Roman law normally considered a slave to be *res,* a thing. But here the master's attitudes transcend the prevailing social norm.

If, then, Luke's redaction included the two groups of emissaries and the accompanying focus on portraying the centurion's positive character traits, then we can also see why Luke speaks of a "slave" *(doulos)* while Matthew speaks of a "child" or "servant" *(pais)*. In the interest of his redactional intentions, Luke alters his source to make the relationship more specific — that of master and slave, while Matthew has preserved the tradition at this point. It is self-evident that a person will be concerned for his sick child, but concern for the health or life of a slave casts a very positive light on the master. At the same time, however, Luke may have altered the ambiguous "child/servant" of his source into a "slave" simply in order to bring the relationship in the story more closely into line with what the centurion says in his statement of faith, where the tradition already used the term "slave" (Matt 8:9; Luke 7:8).

GENRE CRITICISM

The Structure of the Genre

If we have succeeded in identifying Matthew's and Luke's redactional alterations, the version of the story actually passed down to them must emerge. With respect to genre it exhibits the usual features of a miraculous healing: symptoms, petition for healing, words of healing (displaced in Luke by the emissaries), and finally the recognition of the success of the healing. That the miracle worker is not present where the healing takes place can also be identified as a possible topos of miracle stories. Normally "healing at a distance" is used to heighten the sense of the miraculous, but here this topos is the point of departure for the uniqueness of the centurion's confession of faith. The confession attributes to Jesus the power to heal through words alone even though Jesus himself may be physically absent. Although the centurion virtually personifies the illness in his confession of faith, likening it to a soldier or slave, what he says remains within the parameters of the genre, which in accord with its Jewish background regards demonic powers as at work in illnesses.

But healing at a distance is not the focus of the story. That focus is, rather, the centurion's faith. The petitioner's faith is indeed characteristic of New Testament stories of miraculous healing. The supplicant's faith in the miracle worker can be the prerequisite for the actual words of healing (cf. Mark 2:5).

But the way in which this story uses the genre features "healing at a distance" and "petitioner's faith" together transcends the genre of miraculous healings in the strictest sense. The uniqueness of this story is its focus on the particular sort of faith displayed by the centurion, that is, faith in the efficacy of Jesus' words despite his physical absence.

This modification of the genre of miraculous healing manifests itself in another feature of the story as well. Although in other healing stories Jesus mentions faith (cf. Mark 2:5; 5:34), the centurion's faith here prompts Jesus to do what normally only the observers of his miracles do: He responds with astonishment to the centurion's faith. Viewed against the typical genre schema, this reaction actually shifts the miracle story's customary choral conclusion from the astonished crowd to Jesus himself. The real miracle in the story is not the healing but the centurion's faith. So here again the story uses an element typical of the genre, but also alters it and makes it autonomous. Another unique feature here is that the story expressly emphasizes that the petitioner is a Gentile and that his faith exceeded what Jesus found in Israel.

Among other New Testament miracle stories, the one most closely resembling this one is that of the Syrophoenician woman from the Markan tradition (Mark 7:24-30). The Gentile woman humbles herself as the centurion does. Although the story does not focus as explicitly on her faith, Jesus does refer to her words of petition, and again the healing takes place at a distance. It seems that these two stories represent a subgenre of the genre of miraculous healings.

Setting in the Life of the Church and Redactional Setting

That a subgenre is thus represented is shown even more clearly by consideration of the setting of these stories in the life of the church. Although the setting of stories of miraculous healing is generally that of the Christian mission (among Jews, although also among Gentiles), in that the proclamation of Jesus as a miracle worker is intended to motivate faith in him, this is true of the present story only with some qualification. That it is a Gentile who believes in Jesus certainly suggests a missionary situation, particularly because his faith is said to be greater than any found in Israel. But this also means that the story functions less as mission proclamation than as a justification to a Christian audience of acceptance of Gentiles into the church. It could serve as an example of how Jesus himself recognized the Gentile's faith. But the story is not actually about an incident concerning the historical Jesus himself. It deals, rather, with the faith of the post-Easter church: The centurion believes in the efficacy of Jesus' words even when Jesus himself is not physically present, thus anticipating the situation in which the post-Easter church found itself.

Matthew's and Luke's altered uses of this story have also altered its function, thus giving it a "setting in literature." Though the story originally justified the acceptance of Gentiles into the Christian community, this justification was no longer needed by the time of Matthew and Luke.

Matthew's community was a mixture of Jewish and Gentile Christians viewing themselves as the new and true, universally expanded Israel. That community still had contact with Judaism and was in competition with it. That is why Matthew redactionally presents the centurion as a programmatic representative of the Gentiles whose faith gives them access to the true Israel, and this in contrast to the Jews. From his own experience the Gospel writer knew that most Jews were rejecting faith in Jesus, faith that in Matthew's own view is the only thing that can allow them truly to be "Israel."

Luke's church was for the most part a Gentile Christian community. Through their experience of conversion from "God-fearers" to Christians they were able to recognize themselves in the Gentile centurion. Therefore, Luke's redaction shifts the story's accent to the centurion's personality. Luke portrays him as one who is socially aware, who loves his slave, who is generous and respected by others with no loss of humility, and who, not least, has strong faith. Here the miracle recedes even further, and both the petition for healing and the actual words of healing are eliminated. Luke's portrayal thus acquires characteristics of a legend, if by "legend" we understand not an improbable story but a story that depicts a significant person whose positive character traits are exemplary for the readers. Luke proceeds similarly in his Passion narrative: The pious, patiently suffering Jesus becomes a model that the reader is to emulate.

CHAPTER 11

The Healing of a Royal Official's Son
(John 4:46c-54)

John is literarily independent of the Synoptics, even when, as here, he reworks material similar to something found in the Synoptics (see chapter 10 above).[1] Methodologically we find ourselves in the same situation as with Mark: When the original source cannot be established through comparison, as with Matthew and Luke, we must evaluate the consistency or inconsistency of the text after our description of its form. If we do discover inconsistencies in the text, we must make further tradition-critical or source-critical inquiries and then establish through redaction criticism those elements of the text that are the result of redaction.

Only if we succeed in discerning the version handed down to the redactor can we then ask concerning the genre of the original version and its setting in the church's life. This then will enable us both to understand the story before us in the ways it deviates from the genre and to enhance our knowledge of early Christian community life and its historical development.

In vv. 43-55, Jesus returns to Galilee after his initial journey to Jerusalem. V. 46 brings him back to Cana and recalls the miracle performed there earlier. This reference to the earlier miracle and the summary statement in v. 54, which adds the miracle in this story as the "second sign" to the earlier one in Cana, bracket our story. 5:1 then begins a new section with a new journey to Jerusalem.

1. Cf. R. Bultmann, *The Gospel of John: A Commentary*, trans. G. R. Beasley-Murray, et al. (Philadelphia: Westminster, 1971) 204f.

THE FORM OF THE TEXT

The structure of John 4:46-54 is signaled by changes of location, characters, and speaker and by the change from narrative to commentary in v. 54. V. 46 introduces the characters and the location and describes the situation of distress. Vv. 47-50 bring the miracle worker and the petitioner together. Vv. 51-52 confirm the miracle in a dialogue between the petitioner and his servants. V. 53 shows the reaction to the miracle. In v. 54 the narrator offers a summarizing commentary on the events and places the story in the larger narrative context.

John 4:46-54

46		Location, characters, situation of distress
47-50	47	Encounter with the miracle worker, petition for healing (indirect discourse), renewed portrayal of the situation of distress
	48	Jesus' words
	49	Renewed petition for healing and portrayal of the situation of distress
	50a-c	Jesus' words of healing
	50d-f	Petitioner's faith and return
51-52	51	Recognition of success (servants' report of the healing)
	52a-b	Petitioner's question about the hour of healing
	52c-d	Servants' response
53	a-d e	Knowledge of the miracle, reaction to the miracle
54		Narrator's commentary

TENSIONS IN THE TEXT

A number of elements are repeated in the text. Both the beginning (v. 46) and end (v. 54) refer to Cana and to the first miracle performed there.

The petition for healing occurs twice, once in indirect discourse (v. 47) and once in direct discourse (v. 49). The need calling forth this petition is described three times: at the beginning (v. 46), after the first petition (v. 47), and as part of the second petition (v. 49). The second of these descriptions is particularly striking: Although it immediately follows the first petition, it is not part of the petition, but is rather a commentary on the petition. And although its content ("he was at the point of death") agrees with the third description, that third description is in direct discourse ("before my child dies," v. 49).

The petitioner's faith is referred to twice, and it is difficult semantically to explain this repetition without encountering contradictions. According to v. 50 the petitioner believes before knowing of the miracle's success, while according to v. 53 it is knowledge of the miracle's success that brings him to faith.

Furthermore, Jesus' words in v. 48 already speak of faith, though there he addresses the petitioner in the second person *plural*, in contrast to v. 50, where he addresses him in the singular (see the marginal note in NRSV). It may appear from this that Jesus is addressing others in v. 48, though no others are mentioned in the text as it stands.

These observations lead us to suspect that the text is inconsistent, and prompt us to turn to tradition or source criticism.

TRADITION AND SOURCE CRITICISM

The Location of the Healing

The double mention of Cana, the reference to the miracle of the wine, and particularly the enumeration of the miraculous healing as the second sign all lead us to suspect that we may in fact be dealing here more with source criticism than with tradition criticism. That is, the numbering of signs might indicate that the text was not handed down to the redactor as an individual tradition by itself, but rather was already part of a larger, more comprehensive source.

But though 2:11 identifies the miracle of wine at Cana as "the first of his signs" and 4:54 calls the healing the "second sign," other miraculous "signs" performed by Jesus (in Jerusalem) are described between these two, and are not assigned numbers (cf. 2:23). To be sure, in the text as it stands this is not a contradiction, since the healing is in fact the "second sign" *performed in Cana.*

But was Cana the original location of this "second sign"? The story itself mentions that the sick person was at Capernaum, as in the Synoptic version (Matt 8:5; Luke 7:1). After the wine miracle Jesus goes to Capernaum with his disciples and relatives (2:12). But nothing happens there, and the next verse (2:13) takes Jesus to Jerusalem. This makes us wonder why Capernaum is mentioned at all. If it were just a historical footnote, we would expect to hear also of the various stops along the way to Jerusalem. But a short verse (2:13) suffices to account for the eight-day journey (as in 5:1 and 7:10). We can, therefore, suspect that 2:13 interrupts some event in Galilee in order to introduce the whole complex of events that took place in Jerusalem.

It is not difficult, in fact, to append 4:46 directly onto 2:12 or to think that these two verses were, in fact, connected in John's source. In this case Jesus would have gone from Cana to Capernaum and performed the miraculous healing of the official's son there, not in Cana, in keeping with the Synoptics. But the Johannine redactor has Jesus return to Cana after the journey to Jerusalem, not to underscore the motif of healing at a distance, but to associate the miraculous healing more definitely with the miracle of the wine.

Repetitions in the Story

The tension between the two references to the petitioner's faith (vv. 50 and 53) can also be resolved by a distinction between source and redaction. Jesus' words in v. 48 criticize a faith based on visible signs and wonders, though v. 53 then speaks, apparently positively, of just such a faith. But this conflict is resolved if v. 48 is identified as the redactor's corrective addendum. With it, v. 50d-f ("The man believed the word . . .") must also be redactional. V. 53e ("And he himself believed . . .") expresses the source's acceptance of the sort of faith that v. 48 criticizes.

On this basis, we also have an explanation for Jesus' peculiar use of the plural to refer to the petitioner in v. 48. The redactor is thinking not only of the petitioner in the story, but also of his readers: They find themselves in just that situation of having to believe without seeing.

If we thus identify vv. 48 and 50d-f as redactional, then we have also found an explanation for the repeated petition for healing and the three descriptions of the illness. Without Jesus' words in v. 48, which delays the course of the narrative, there would be no need to repeat the petition in

v. 49. But which of the two petitions belongs to the original source? The discourse introduction before the petition for healing in direct discourse (v. 49) uses the historic present tense (literally "the official *says* to him"), as does the discourse introduction in v. 50 ("Jesus *says* to him"). So we may assume that this is the petition from the source and that the petition in v. 47 is redactional. This redactional addition was necessitated by the insertion of Jesus' statement in v. 48. This would also explain why the petition is introduced in v. 47 in the past tense, rather than the historic present, and why it is in indirect rather than direct discourse. It also explains why it is said twice that the child is about to die (vv. 47, 49).

The Original Form of the Story

If this reconstruction of the relation of source and redaction is on target, then the story as it appeared in the source was as follows: After the miracle of the wine Jesus went to Capernaum (2:12), where an official's son was sick. The official came to Jesus and asked him to heal his son. Jesus uttered the words of healing. Then the man left, met his servants on the way home, learned from them the hour of the healing, and recognized that it occurred at the hour in which Jesus was speaking the words of healing. Then "he himself believed, and all his household." In conclusion the source identifies this miracle as "the second sign that Jesus did."

The Johannine Source and Q

This pre-Johannine story was not literarily dependent on the Synoptic story of the centurion of Capernaum. But there are similarities, particularly with the Matthean version, which, as we saw in chapter 10, stands closer to Q than Luke does in this story. Matthew does not make it clear whether it is the centurion's "child" or "servant" who is ill, and in John or his source it is the official's "son" (v. 46) or "child" (v. 49). Both Matthew and John include with the petition a portrayal of symptoms (Matt 8:6; John 4:49), both include with the words of healing an order to depart (Matt 8:13; John 4:50), and both use the address "Lord" (Matt 8:8; John 4:49). Matthew mentions the "hour" of healing (Matt 8:13), which John 4:51-53 elaborately employs in its sequence concerning the confirmation of healing.

The Johannine version shares with the Lukan version that the ill person is "at the point of death" (Luke 7:2; John 4:47, 49). Finally, John's source shares with both Synoptics the location of the healing (Capernaum), the element of healing at a distance, and the motif of faith.

From all this it appears that the Johannine story was related at some stage of transmission with the Synoptic story. This can be explained in two different ways: Perhaps a textual unit in oral tradition was incorporated into Q and also found its way — quite independently of Q — into the milieu of traditions within which the Johannine source was composed:

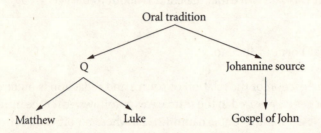

Or perhaps, within the milieu of traditions used as the source for the Gospel of John, the Synoptics (or one of them) were also familiar, if not in written form then possibly through oral recitation, perhaps in worship services. As such they might have served as the point of departure for a newly emerging oral tradition that ultimately reached its written form in the Johannine source:

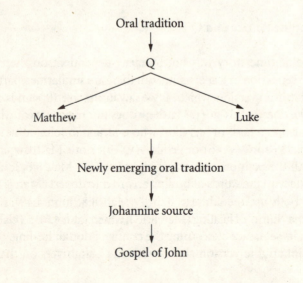

But there are, of course, differences between the story in the Johannine source and the Synoptics' account. The most prominent difference is that the problem of Jewish-Gentile relationships plays no prominent role in the Johannine story, though it does in the Synoptic story.

Other important differences are found in relation to the motif of faith. In the Synoptics faith is itself the real miracle. But in John's source faith arises only as a result of the miracle. In the Synoptics the motif of healing at a distance serves only to throw the centurion's unique faith into relief. In John's source the motif of healing at a distance has become autonomous. As shown particularly by the elaborately developed sequence concerning the confirmation of healing in the dialogue between the official and his servants (John 4:51-53), the spectacular healing at a distance is virtually the center of the story. These differences direct us to the question of the genre of John's source.

GENRE CRITICISM

John's original source, thus established by the methods of tradition criticism, exhibits typical features of the miracle genre, specifically of the genre of stories of miraculous healing: The situation of distress is described, the supplicant approaches the miracle worker and gives his petition for healing, the miracle worker speaks words of healing, the success of the healing is recognized, and some reaction to the events is described.

Within this genre John's source is particularly striking in its prominent use of the motif of healing at a distance. In contrast with the Synoptics, who frequently use the miracle stories to reveal the substance of the kingdom of God proclaimed by Jesus, the portrayal in John focuses on the miracle worker and his extraordinary abilities. Accordingly, the story itself moves toward its goal of eliciting faith in him as a figure equipped with divine gifts.

We can thus say more unequivocally than ever that the "miracle story" is an instrument of mission[2] and that it thus found its setting in

2. M. Dibelius, *From Tradition to Gospel*, trans. B. L. Woolf (New York: Scribner, n.d.) 96.

115

the service of religious propaganda.[3] The source as a whole had the same setting, as is shown by the juxtaposition of spectacular and impressive miracles and their enumeration as "signs."

On the basis of this designation of Jesus' miracles as "signs," scholars have called this presumed source of the Gospel of John the "signs" source.[4] If this source was indeed a collection of spectacular miracle stories, then its setting was the Christian mission and its goal was to elicit faith in Jesus by telling of the deeds by which he outdid all other miracle workers.

But the source thus ran the risk of identifying Jesus as one among the many miracle workers familiar in antiquity. It could thus lose his unique claim among the multiplicity of religious systems and doctrines of salvation and make of the gospel of Christ just a report of another miracle worker. And it could lead readers to forget in docetic fashion[5] that the son of God is Jesus of Nazareth, or, in John's words, that the Logos became flesh and is not to be thought of merely as a *theios anēr*, as a semi-divine being among the other well-known phenomena of religious history. For this reason, the Johannine redaction can be understood as a corrective to the source.

REDACTION CRITICISM

V. 48 makes it clear that this is the case. This verse has no function in the course of the story: Jesus' address does not direct itself to the

---

3. Jesus himself understood his own deeds — deeds transcending the sphere of daily life — as genuine signs showing *how* the kingdom that he proclaimed as commencing would change the circumstances of the present age, and showing *that* this kingdom was about to bring about that change. But the miracle story in John's source relates an event that as a legitimizing "sign" draws attention to Jesus himself and seeks to motivate or even prompt faith in him. It is in keeping with this goal that the element of the miraculous — here the motif of healing at a distance — is heightened and placed at the center of the story. The narrator's goal here is to elicit faith in Jesus in a missionary situation, as shown especially by the formulation "and he himself believed, and all his household." We may view this as a phrase from missionary language referring to conversion to Christianity, a phrase from a period in which a person joined the Christian community with his household.

4. See above, p. 49, n. 7.

5. Docetism was a denial of the humanity and sufferings of Christ sometimes accomplished by a distinction between the heavenly Christ and the earthly Jesus.

petitioning father, but speaks rather in the plural, which includes the readers: "Unless you (plural) see signs and wonders, you (plural) will not believe." This sentence is a clear criticism of the concept of faith exemplified by the old miracle story (in v. 53). Before believing, a person insists on assurances. If such a person cannot first see, he or she is unable to believe and resembles Thomas, who insisted on seeing the print of the nails in the hands of the resurrected Jesus as a prerequisite to faith (20:25). But Jesus rejects a faith that depends exclusively on visible signs and wonders.

Faith arising only from visible, spectacular miracles is no faith at all, since miracles are always equivocal; a person does not come to faith simply by seeing the signs (cf. 6:26). Rather, faith arises where a person believes the word that Jesus has spoken (4:50). That word proclaims life and is accepted in faith.

Why, then, did the redactor not eliminate the tension between faith prior to the miracle and faith elicited by the miracle? The redactor left the reference to faith elicited by the miracle (4:53) because in this way the man in the story is portrayed as encountering the miracle as a believer. As a believer, he recognizes the real meaning of the miracle, so that it discloses itself to him in a fashion that prompts yet another stage of faith. He does not believe in Jesus merely as a miracle worker — even as the greatest among miracle workers — but rather through faith sees in Jesus the one who is the true salvation and deliverance from death.

CHAPTER 12

Two Christological Hymns
(Phil 2:6-11; 1 Tim 3:16)

The New Testament does not have its own special collection of prayers of the kind found in the Psalter of the Hebrew Bible. The early Christians used the Psalter itself as their prayer book and quite unaffectedly understood the psalms to be speaking about Christ. Yet at a very early period there did arise individual Christian prayers of the kind that the author of the letter to the Colossians may have had in mind when he exhorts his community to "sing psalms and hymns and spiritual songs with thankfulness in your hearts to God" (Col 3:16).[1]

Like the Song of Hannah (1 Samuel 2:1-10) or David's beautiful lament over Saul and Jonathan (2 Samuel 1:17-27) in the Hebrew Bible, every hymn in the New Testament is, of course, preserved as part of a larger writing. For example, the Gospel of Luke contains the Magnificat and the Benedictus (Luke 1:46-55, 68-79). New Testament hymns speak frequently of God's saving acts in Christ. They refer to Christ in the third person and are thus in the form of proclamation rather than being addressed to God or Christ. This made it easier for them to find use in the didactic sections of the New Testament letters. This utilization of the hymns gave them, nonetheless, a new "setting in literature." The interpreter must strictly distinguish between the use of a hymn and its original intention.

Tradition and redaction criticism show us, for instance, that Paul

---

1. Ephesians represents a later stage in this development that takes this exhortation in Colossians as speaking of praise of Christ (Eph 5:19), though the New Testament does not yet attest prayers or songs specifically addressed to Christ.

is citing a hymn that he himself has not composed in Phil 2:6-11. He does so in order to base the ethical imperatives he is presenting to the community on the indicative of salvation. The moral obligations of Christians are always rooted in Christian existence, an existence that Christ has redeemed.

The author of 1 Timothy also cites an already existing christological hymn, but does so in order to give the community a corrective guide to true Christian faith in the post-apostolic period of emerging false doctrines. He believes that the apostle himself already formulated such a guide in language that transcends the ages.

We must thus distinguish between, on the one hand, what the hymns themselves say, including what effect they have through the genre to which they belong and their setting in the church's life, and, on the other hand, what the redactors intend when, by citing the hymns and altering them, they give them a "setting in literature."

The Hymn in Philippians

Form and Tradition Criticism[2]

Phil 2:6-11 differs stylistically from its context, which is characterized by direct address and imperatives. Second person plural imperatives occur in vv. 2 and 5 and then in vv. 12 and 14. In vv. 6-11 we see narrative statements in the third person, that is, statements about the one identified at the end as Jesus Christ.

Like the psalms of the Hebrew Bible, the New Testament hymns also make use of the traditional stylistic devices of Semitic poetry. Indeed, the role that parallelism plays in the structure of the Philippians hymn is so decisive that it transcends even the concerns of form criticism and enables our tradition and redaction criticism to distinguish the original hymn from Paul's interpretative additions. The parts of the text printed in italics in our diagram of the hymn so disrupt the paral-

---

2. We will abbreviate our procedure here by beginning with a form-critical look at the text that has already been established as original. That is, we will ignore the parts of the text printed in italics, which are in tension with the structure of the text and are presumed to be Pauline additions.

Philippians 2:6-11

A	I	a	6 He who was in the form of God did not count equality with God a thing to be grasped,
		b	7 but emptied himself,
			taking the form of a servant,
		c	being born in human likeness.
	II	a′	*And being found in human appearance,
		b′	8 he humbled himself
		c′	and became obedient to death,
			even death on a cross.
B		x	9 Therefore God has **highly** exalted him
		x′	and bestowed on him the name which is **high above every** name,
		y	10 so that at the name of Jesus **every** knee should bow, in heaven, on earth, and under the earth,
		y′	11 and **every** tongue confess that "Jesus Christ is Lord,"
			to the glory of God the Father.

*V. 8 begins with this line in English versions.

lelism of the other lines that they destroy the structural consistency of the text and must be viewed as later additions of the author who is citing the hymn, namely, Paul. If we read the text without these additions, the parallelism between the text's components and their macro-structural arrangement are easily discernible and give the text the character of a consciously formed poetic text.

The change of subject in v. 9 indicates where the hymn is divided into two sections (A and B). Christ is the subject from v. 6 to v. 8, even if he is not mentioned specifically by name, but rather, in the typical fashion of New Testament christological hymns, by the indefinite relative pronoun "who." God is the subject in vv. 9-11.

The first section (A), which speaks of what Christ experiences, is subdivided into two segments describing sequential stages of that experience. This subdivision is suggested by the parallelism of the two segments: The beginning of segment A.I makes a statement about Christ's manner of existence in his preexistence "in the form of God." This parallels the beginning of segment A.II, which speaks of Christ's manner of existence "in human appearance" (a/a′).

The activity of the preexisting Christ in the form of God and of Christ in his human appearance also parallel one another: His self-emptying (b) corresponds to his self-humiliation (b'). In the first he voluntarily surrenders the form of God, and in the second he willingly gives up his human appearance. Each time this transfers him to a lower stage: The two stages of this freely accepted path (c/c') lead him from the form of God to human likeness, and from this human appearance to obedient acceptance of death.

The text's second sequence (B), which we have already recognized from the change of subject, follows as a conclusion from the first. Christ obeyed in his surrender of divine form, his assumption of human appearance, and his acceptance of death. *Therefore* God acted to compensate Christ.

God's action on Christ's behalf is twofold and is described in two parallel clauses:

> Therefore God has **highly** exalted him
> and bestowed on him the name which is **high above** every name.
> (x/x')

The twofold goal of this action is described in the following parallel dependent ("so that") clauses:

> So that . . . **every** knee should bow . . . ,
> and **every** tongue confess. . . . (y/y')

These two pairs of internally parallel statements are also chiastically related to one another: The bestowal of the name above *every* name (x') corresponds to the statement that "at the name of Jesus *every* knee should bow" (y); similarly, it is appropriate that God's "exaltation" of Jesus (x) be expressed in the confession "Jesus Christ is Lord" (y').

Redaction Criticism

As we have noted, the parts of the text printed in italics, that is, the second clause of v. 7 and the last lines of vv. 8 and 11, disturb the parallel structure of this hymn. These lines were added as a theological corrective, probably by Paul. Without them, there is a greater risk of understanding Christ's double descent as merely apparent. The Christ praised in the hymn would, then, take only an illusory path from the divine to the human sphere and thence to the sphere of death, in such a way that he is not in himself affected by this descent at all.

In fact, a Gnostic mythological idea of a divine being appears to lie behind the original form of the hymn. This divine being descends from its heavenly sphere into the material sphere of the world in order to rescue the divine seeds or sparks trapped in that world during a primordial catastrophe and to lead them back into the heavenly world. The divine being itself is not, however, really affected by this descent. It assumes the form of the inhabitants of each successive sphere only as a disguise so that hostile powers cannot recognize it.

The Pauline additions to the hymn rescue it from this kind of (mis)understanding. Christ, in the form of God and having descended from God's sphere, did not simply disguise himself as a human being; rather, he "took the form of a servant," that is, the countenance and fate of the suffering servant of God who atones for the many (Isaiah 53). Paul, the missionary to the Gentiles, was doubtlessly thoroughly familiar with this figure from the prophetic proclamation of deutero-Isaiah.

Paul also understands Christ's obedient acceptance of death as neither simply an accommodation to the fate ordained for all humankind nor as an event that does not really affect Christ. The crucified Christ has neither peacefully passed away nor suffered merely the "apparent" death described in the Gnostic myth, whose redeemer figure uses death as the most sublime disguise. Rather, the one spoken of in the hymn is Jesus of Nazareth, whose obedience to the Father extended to death itself, "even death on a cross," that is, to the bloody and shameful execution of a criminal forsaken even by God.

Finally, though Paul could agree fully with the confession "Jesus Christ is Lord," he did not see Christ's lordship as displacing God himself — as would be the case in the Gnostic myth with its idea of the ultimate triumph of the good redeemer god of love over the evil creator god. For Paul, even the lordship of the exalted Christ performs a service: Its ultimate (apocalyptic) goal is to deliver the kingdom to the Father so that God "may be all in all" (1 Cor 15:24, 28). Therefore, Paul once again *theo*logically qualifies the acclamation of the powers "in heaven, on earth, and under the earth" to Jesus Christ the Lord. In the final analysis, Christ's lordship is "to the glory of God the Father," not for the sake of perfecting his own standing.

THE HYMN IN 1 TIMOTHY

Form Criticism

The hymn in 1 Tim 3:16 is introduced by a citation formula with a neuter subject ("mystery"), which is thus distinguished grammatically from the masculine relative pronoun "who" that follows (cf. the text-critical observations above, pp. 18-20): "Great, indeed, as is known to all, is the mystery of our religion, who

1. was manifested in the flesh,
2. was justified in the Spirit,
3. appeared to angels,
4. was preached among the nations,
5. was believed on in the world,
6. was taken up in glory."

The conclusion of the hymn is also clearly marked, since a new theme is introduced in 4:1.

The text is composed of six clauses with one subject, the relative pronoun "who." These clauses are almost perfect parallels syntactically. Each clause except the third begins with a third person singular verb in the passive voice. The third line has a middle voice verb, which is externally similar to the passive verbs. Every verb except the third is qualified by an adverbial phrase of location using the Greek preposition *en* ("in" or "among") with a noun in the dative case. The third line has a dative noun with no preposition ("to angels"), which is also to be understood as referring to location, as indicating, that is, the location of the "appearance" of the Christ praised in the hymn.

These indications of location in the six clauses can be arranged in groups: In lines 1, 2, 5, and 6 the dative nouns are singular, and in lines 3 and 4 they are plural. The six syntactically parallel lines are thus arranged in three groups of two lines each. This is confirmed semantically by "flesh" and "Spirit" in the first two lines, which are a conceptual pair pointing respectively to the earthly sphere of humans and the heavenly sphere of God. The same sort of contrast is found also in the other two pairs of lines: "angels" vs. "nations" and "world" vs. "(heavenly) glory."

But these contrasting terms point not to an antithetical relation-

123

ship, one in which the differences between the opposing quantities are emphasized, but rather to a polar relationship. That is, the contrasting elements are conceived as the two poles of a single reality. The goal of what is said in the hymn is to bring as much of that reality as possible to expression. The totality of the earthly and heavenly spheres is affected by the Christ event.

The sequence of these spheres within the hymn's text, that is, of the adverbial phrases of location, is also significant. If we designate the earthly sphere with "A" and the heavenly sphere with "B," we see that the six lines are placed in parallel and chiastic arrangements:

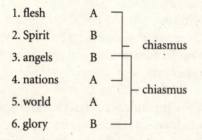

1. flesh	A
2. Spirit	B
		chiasmus
3. angels	B
4. nations	A
		chiasmus
5. world	A
6. glory	B

This confirms what was said earlier, namely, that the text is arranged in three segments of two lines each.

The meanings of the verbs in these six lines further underscore this arrangement in three pairs. Despite differences in meaning between the verbs in each pair, at a more abstract level each verb has one of two semantic elements. In lines 1, 3, and 4 the verbs refer in different ways to proclamation. The verbs in lines 2, 5, and 6 refer in different ways to acceptance of this announcement. How the tripartite arrangement is confirmed from the perspective of these verbal concepts is evident in this schematic overview:

1. proclamation	synthetic parallelism
2. acceptance	
3. proclamation	synonymous parallelism
4. proclamation	
5. acceptance	synonymous parallelism
6. acceptance	

There is no chiastic arrangement as there is with the adverbial phrases. But the semantic parallelism of the verbs establishes a certain order. The verbs in 1 and 2 exhibit synthetic parallelism: Together they encompass the entire process of earthly incarnation and heavenly exaltation. But lines 3 through 6 consist of two pairs in synonymous parallelism. Lines 1 and 2 are thus more complex semantically than lines 3 and 4 or lines 5 and 6.

We can see the consequences this has for interpretation if we consider the verbs and adverbial phrases together. Lines 1 and 2 encompass the entire Christ event. The incarnation ("manifested in the flesh") takes place in the earthly sphere, while the exaltation, through which God "justifies" or accepts Christ, takes place in the heavenly sphere of the "Spirit." The following two pairs of lines develop the results of this Christ event in both heaven and earth: The incarnate and exalted Christ is introduced to the inhabitants of the heavenly sphere ("angels") and of the earthly sphere ("nations") as their Lord (lines 3 and 4). As such he is accepted both on earth and in (heavenly) "glory" (lines 5 and 6). Heaven and earth thus constitute a unity grounded in the Christ event, which affects or encompasses both spheres.

For the author of this christological hymn, who believes in Jesus as the incarnate one who has been taken up to God, the events of Christ's revelation in the flesh and of his justification in the Spirit together ground this unity of heaven and earth. Or more precisely it is God himself, acting in Jesus on earth and then in heaven, who grounds this unity.

Redaction Criticism

Our form-critical description has shown that this is a text composed with such a high degree of formal structure that we can find no trace of tension in it and therefore no point of departure for distinguishing between the original tradition and possible redactional alterations. The text's formal compactness, especially when compared to the text surrounding it, leads us, rather, to conclude that the author is citing a traditional text essentially as it was handed down. (Genre-critical observations also support this conclusion. The hymn's style, particularly the way it begins with the relative pronoun "who" — with no antecedent — and its parallel semantic structures indicate that it belongs to the genre of "hymn.") To determine the redactional intentions of the author citing the hymn we must look at its context.

The hymn occurs in this fictitious letter at an important turning point that is part of the overall epistolary framework. With 3:14-16 the author brings to a close the section of the letter dealing with church regulations, including instructions concerning the conduct of men, women, and officials of the church (2:1–3:13). The same three verses open a section written to combat heresy (4:1ff.). At this turning point the figure of the fictitious author, "Paul," emerges more prominently: "I am writing this to you in the hope that I will come to you soon" (3:14). This is intended to put the stamp of apostolic authority on the preceding regulations. The citation of a traditional hymn in v. 16 is intended to show in this context that the post-apostolic church possesses the apostolic "truth" (3:15) and "sound doctrine" (1:10). When the need arises, the church can cite this doctrine in the form in which it was handed down, that is, in the form going back to the apostles, in the hymn.

But this changes the function of the hymn. As a hymn it shared the liturgical setting of hymns in general, but now it is cited as an example of the "sound doctrine" and apostolic "truth" to which the church of the Pastoral Epistles claims to have access. As such it is a confession of faith more than a hymn. The adverb in the citation formula represented in English by the phrase "as is known to all" introduces the hymn in the present context and draws attention to this alteration of function; the verb "confess" (Greek *homologeō*) would be heard behind this rare adverb *(homologoumenōs).*

Since the hymn has become a confession of faith, it now has the function of such confessions. As "the mystery of our religion" it is now the "truth" revealed to the church and given over to its safekeeping — the "truth" passed down to the church from the apostle as tradition to be nurtured and defended as the criterion distinguishing true "religion" from heresy. The "later times" in which "some will depart from the faith by giving heed to deceitful spirits and doctrines of demons" (4:1) have begun with the author's post-apostolic generation. Therefore, he invokes the figure of the apostle Paul in a fictional epistolary framework and cites the traditional hymn as the central statement of apostolic doctrine. In this way the context in which the hymn is placed, rather than any alterations of the hymn, shows what the author's intentions were.

126

THE GENRE OF THE HYMNS

Despite their differences, the two texts we have discussed share enough common elements of form and content to characterize them as belonging to the same genre. We can see here that a "genre" is an ideal or typical form that is never completely realized in the representatives of the genre.[3] A genre does not exist independently, but is the result of a process of abstraction, in which we must give more weight to some formal features than to others.

Both texts we have been examining begin with a relative pronoun with no antecedent, which is a stylistic feature characteristic of their genre (cf. Col 1:15, 18; Heb 1:3; 1 Pet 2:22; 3:22). In each case, statements concerning the unnamed person represented by the relative pronoun are in the third person and deal with deeds which that person has performed. And both texts use parallelism, which we have discussed as a stylistic feature of poetry influenced by the Hebrew Bible and by the New Testament's Semitic environment (see above, pp. 33-35).

The two texts also contain elements of content that are similar, the most important being incarnation and exaltation. Both texts also mention the subjugation of angelic powers, indeed of all creation, to the unnamed person in the text, though the deeds described make it obvious that the person is to be identified as Christ. All these common features constitute what we may call the style of this genre.[4]

The genre of a text gives us clues concerning how the text functioned. That these texts describe Christ's deeds in the third person suggests that they are thus intended as a report to a third party. Since the subject's name is not mentioned, we can assume that these texts

---

3. A certain vagueness thus invariably characterizes the term "genre." The structural criteria that unite the forms of individual texts into a genre are used in the individual texts with greater or lesser degrees of thoroughness. Furthermore, there is a hierarchy of genre terms extending from the larger categories of prose, poetry, narrative, and argumentative texts all the way down to groups of texts in which the syntactic structure is virtually identical. Despite this vagueness, the term "genre" has much pragmatic usefulness.

4. Individual features emerge in addition to these shared elements. 1 Tim 3:16 interprets the subjugation of the angelic powers and the human world as a missionary event, while Phil 2:6-11 sees it as a heavenly enthronement. Phil 2:6-11 dedicates an entire strophe (the first) to Christ's heavenly preexistence, but 1 Tim 3:16 does not explicitly mention preexistence, though it can be inferred from the statement concerning incarnation.

were originally used in a larger context that made it clear who the unnamed subject is. That statements are made about only one subject (Christ) shows the significance that the authors of these texts ascribed to Christ's deeds and life for the intended addressees. And the thoroughgoing poetic structuring of the texts elevates the information above the level of daily life and suggests that they are directed not to a single addressee, but rather to a larger circle.

The initial relative pronoun points to influence by Semitic prayer texts. This suggests that the context of these texts, in which the addressees would learn who is meant by the relative pronoun, was probably liturgical. The genre functions liturgically, therefore: Its setting in the church's life is the worship service, in which praise of Christ's person and redemptive acts becomes, in the congregation's singing, praise of the exalted Lord. But such praise, being stated in the third person, was also proclamation. For this reason texts of this genre could easily acquire a secondary setting through literary use, as did the two hymns we have examined.

In Phil 2:6-11 Paul cites a hymn in order to ground the parenetic imperative, that is, the church's ethical obligations, in the christological indicative — in the church's relationship to Christ. The author of 1 Timothy cites a traditional hymn as an example of the apostolic doctrine by which the post-apostolic church has access to the truth. The hymn praising Christ thus becomes a confession of faith. It is not surprising, then, to learn that the genre of the traditional text in 1 Tim 3:16 has been identified in a number of ways: Scholars speak here of a "confession of faith," "hymn," "song," "liturgical confession formula," "symbolum apostolicum," "early Christian song," "confessional song," "confession-like song to the redeemer," "liturgical confession," etc.

Although the biblical authors established and used many different genres, they did not develop fixed terms for genres. Use of genres is different from abstract identification of them. The "psalms, hymns, and spiritual odes" of Col 3:16 and the "psalms, hymns, and odes" of Eph 5:19 are not precise or fixed designations. Both passages seem to be speaking a plerophoric language that indicates its subject by multiplication of terms rather than by precise designation. Though the New Testament thus uses various genre designations for liturgical texts, we associate the designation "psalm" too specifically with the texts (of various genres) collected in the Hebrew Psalter. And when we hear the term "ode," we sooner think of the odes of Horace or John Keats.

Therefore, "hymn" is probably the most useful designation for the genre represented in Phil 2:6-11 and 1 Tim 3:16 — or perhaps, more specifically, "christological hymn," to distinguish these texts from others that are better described as "hymns to God." But we can forego the further specification "christological hymn of proclamation," since all the New Testament christological hymns are in the form of third-person proclamations. Christological hymns of adoration and imprecation in direct address emerge only after the New Testament.

THE TRADITIONAL IDEA OF PREEXISTENCE

The first strophe of Phil 2:6-11 deals with an idea that also seems implied in the first line of the hymn in 1 Tim 3:16, an idea we can regard as an established theme, that is, as a "tradition." This is the idea of Jesus' preexistence. By "preexistence" we mean that before Jesus' birth or earthly appearance — indeed, even before creation — he resided with God as the "Son of God," as the "word" *(logos)*, or in the "manner of divine existence"; God even created the world "in him" ("mediator of creation") in order to send him into the world in the end time.

Paul uses this concept as unaffectedly as the Gospel of John, but the Synoptic tradition seems to get along without it. The hymnic material that Paul cites in Philippians 2 shows that it was already an established theme. A schema occurring twice in Paul and three times in the Johannine writings helps to illuminate the tradition history of the idea:

Gal 4:4a When the time had fully come,
     b *God sent* his *Son*,
     c born of a woman,
     d born under the law,
    5a *so that* he might redeem those who were under the law,
     b *so that* we might receive adoption as sons.

Rom 8:3a What the law could not do,
     b weakened by the flesh,
     c *God* has done:
     d *sending* his own *Son* in the likeness of sinful flesh and
       for the sake of sinners
     e he condemned sin in the flesh,

> 4a *in order that* the just requirements of the law might be
>   fulfilled in us,
> b who walk not according to the flesh but according to the Spirit.

> John 3:16a *God* so loved the world
>   b that he *gave* his only *Son,*
>   c *so that* whoever believes in him should not perish
>   d but have eternal life.

> John 3:17a *God sent* the *Son* into the world,
>   b not *so that* he might condemn the world,
>   c but rather *so that* the world might be saved through him.

> 1 John 4:9a In this the love of God was made manifest among us,
>   b that *God sent* his only *Son* into the world,
>   c *so that* we might live through him.

The constant structure visible in these passages is this: The acting subject is God, who sends or gives. What he sends is always his (or the) Son. And a purpose clause ("so that") indicates the soteriological purpose of this sending. Both Paul and John acquired this christological schema from tradition and used it for their own contextual purposes.

This schema is also discernible in a passage from the Wisdom of Solomon:

> Wis 9:9a With you, *God,* is *wisdom.*
>   b She knows your works
>   c and was present
>   d when you made the world.
>   e She understands what is pleasing in your sight
>   and what is right according to your commandments.
>   10a *Send* her forth from the holy heavens,
>   b and from the throne of your glory *send* her,
>   c *that* she may be with me and toil,
>   d and *that* I may learn what is pleasing in you.

Here "wisdom" replaces "the Son" as the object of the sending, and the sending is not thought of as having occurred in the past; it is, rather, requested in prayer for the future. Since this passage is older than those from the New Testament, the schema was probably not originally christological. It was already used in Jewish texts: "Wisdom" was already thought of as preexistent.

Wisdom literature originated in Hellenistically influenced Jewish circles in Egypt. In the Hellenistic environment it was recognized that not just in Israel but also among Gentiles were found values, virtues, and insights that Israel had earlier viewed as the fruit of the divine law given only to it. This recognition was apparently seen as a problem: How could Israel maintain its identity and avoid denying its tradition of faith — and the divine law that set Israel apart as the chosen people — and still remain open to this Gentile wisdom, which was valuable and in many respects agreed with Israel's law?

The idea of wisdom's preexistence was an attempt to resolve this dilemma. Preexistent wisdom transcends any particular form of wisdom. God created the world in this wisdom. Therefore, the world itself, as an intelligible creation open to the insight of all peoples, could be the source of the wisdom of all. Israel has its special status because God gave wisdom to Israel in a special way in the law at Sinai. So although wisdom is discernible everywhere in creation, it dwells in a special way in the tents of Jacob.

This solution to the problem of the relationship between particularism and universalism also eliminated another problem. Because people began thinking less in historical terms — again under the influence of Greek thought — and were more inclined to develop ideas in spatial terms, God receded further and further from humanity into inaccessible spheres and disappeared more and more within transcendence. To speak of God's acts on earth, one referred, then, to his wisdom, word, or power, which became more and more thought of as separate divine beings. By referring to them, one could express the conviction, held by those of steadfast faith in God's greatness and inaccessibility, that God was nonetheless concerned with human beings and that he acts in history.

We can now understand why Christians from this Hellenistic Jewish tradition did not, as did Jewish Christians from Palestine, refer to Jesus as "Messiah" to express their belief that he was the ultimate redeemer and that in him, in his deeds, words, and cross, God had acted eschatologically for the salvation of all humankind. Rather, they spoke of him as the preexistent wisdom, the Logos, the Son whom God had sent into the world.

By referring to preexistence they could also differentiate the incomparable and final sending of Christ from that of the prophets, who also understood themselves as sent. And Hellenistic Christians could also in this way proclaim the relevance of the redeeming Christ event

131

for the entire Gentile world, since preexistence does, after all, imply the mediation of creation itself. One could thus say that the world was created in the preexistent Jesus, that is, as a world oriented from the very outset toward redemption in Christ, redemption that thus also includes Gentiles. No wonder, then, that Paul, the apostle to the Gentiles, made use of this preexistence christology. And when Hellenistic Christians wanted to express the hope for a future revelation of meaning, hope that their experience of Jesus had ignited in them, they could hardly begin from the proposition that the present age came merely out of chaotic meaninglessness. Therefore, they spoke of God having created this world in his own Son, the eternal Logos, having as the object of their hope a God who desires the fellowship of all humankind.

CHAPTER 13

The Genealogy of Jesus According to Matthew (Matt 1:1-25)

The beginnings and ends of ancient books are especially significant in interpreting the books, so it is appropriate for us to analyze at least one such beginning. The genealogy of Jesus at the beginning of Matthew's Gospel also has the advantage of giving us the opportunity to work with a biblical list. In this way we can learn something further about methodology, since in an apparently monotonous list both what is repeated and what is unique to a given item on the list are perhaps more noticeable than in other kinds of texts.

In Matt 1:1 the genealogy of Jesus begins with the beginning of the Gospel. That something new begins in 2:1 is indicated by the introduction of the place, time, and characters, some of them mentioned by name, of the narrative in ch. 2. That 1:18-25 belongs to the genealogy can be seen by the repetition of the Greek word *genesis* in 1:18 (rendered in RSV and NRSV as "genealogy" in 1:1 and as "birth" in 1:18) and by the reintroduction of the name "Jesus Christ," which last occurred in 1:16.

THE FORM OF THE TEXT

In this text we can distinguish:[1]

---

1. Following A. Vögtle, "Die Genealogie Mt 1,2-26 und die matthäische Kindheitsgeschichte (II)," *Biblische Zeitschrift* 8 (1964) 240.

1. the superscription (v. 1),
2. the genealogy (vv. 2-16),
3. a commentary on the genealogy as a whole (v. 17), and
4. an excursus on v. 16 that tells of the birth of Christ (vv. 18-25).

The genealogy itself can be further subdivided in this way:

Matthew 1:2ff.

I	2a Abraham was the father of Isaac,
	  b and Isaac the father of Jacob,
	  c and Jacob the father of Judah and his brothers,

	3a and Judah the father of Perez and Zerah by Tamar, b and Perez the father of Hezron . . . 5a and Salmon the father of Boaz by Rahab,
	b and Boaz the father of Obed by Ruth, c and Obed the father of Jesse, 6a and Jesse the father of David the king.
II	b and David was the father of Solomon by the wife of Uriah, 7a and Solomon the father of Rehoboam . . . 11a and Josiah the father of Jechoniah and his brothers, at the time of the deportation to Babylon.

III	12a And after the deportation to Babylon:
	Jechoniah was the father of Salathiel . . .
	16a and Jacob the father of Joseph
	  b the husband of Mary,
	  c of whom Jesus was born,
	  d who is called Christ.

While the genealogy is narrative in form, the superscription and commentary are not strictly narrative but discursive, referring to what is narrated in the genealogy. One can thus understand them as "metanarrative statements," that is, as guides to show the reader how the narrative of the genealogy is to be read. Statements are "metanarrative" if they treat the narrator, the one who reads or hears the narrative, and the narrative situation as themes for discussion. Both of the metanarrative statements here, the superscription (v. 1) and the commentary (v. 17), seek to draw the reader's attention to the genealogy and give special emphasis to something that the genealogy is saying.

The superscription and the commentary go in reverse directions: Abraham → David → Christ vs. Christ → David → Abraham. The superscription speaks of Jesus' "sonship in Abraham" by looking backward through the generations. The commentary looks forward through the generations: Beginning with Abraham, it traces the genealogical line in three groups of fourteen generations each from Abraham to David, to the Babylonian exile, and finally to the goal of the genealogy, Jesus Christ. But this counting of the generations contradicts the text of the genealogy itself. The genealogy does mention the same three temporal divisions, but the first and third include only thirteen progenitors each. The middle section lists fourteen progenitors. So the commentary's ascription of fourteen generations to each division is accurate only if the first and third include the son of the final father in each list, that is David and — in a modified fashion — Jesus.

This contradiction between commentary and genealogy draws special attention to David and Jesus and relates these two men to one another. Furthermore, the attribution of special titles only to these two persons also lends them more significance than the others in the list ("David the king," v. 6; "Jesus, who is called Christ," v. 16). These "titles" are particularly conspicuous because they add something to the repeated schema of "and x the father of y." The microstructure of the genealogy is indicated by these and other interruptions of the genealogical schema.

The first such interruption occurs in v. 2c: Not just one son is mentioned, but rather "Judah and his brothers." This may simply be fortuitous, except that in the immediately following statement we encounter yet another interruption of the schema: Judah, like Jacob, is presented not as the procreator of a single son, but of two, mentioned by name along with their mother (v. 3a). V. 5a and v. 5b also mention mothers by name.

If we take these interruptions of the normal form as signals for division of the text, the first section of the genealogy according to the commentary in v. 17, the generations from Abraham to David, can be subdivided into three shorter textual components, the first including three generations, the second seven, and the third three again. The symbolic significance of these two numbers in the Bible suggests that this is no accident, and this becomes clearer if we consider the theology of history behind this arrangement: First come the three patriarchs Abraham, Isaac, and Jacob, the recipients of God's promise to Israel. David, as the father standing at the end of the series of three commenc-

135

ing with Obed and Ruth, is the king of Israel by divine calling. In both cases, "wherever God is at work we often encounter threefold calling or repetition."[2]

And it is not accidental that the first period of national history — from the exodus to the conquest — is represented by seven generations. The number seven "is associated with the Semitic idea of fullness, completeness, and of a temporal span in its entirety,"[3] and exhibits the character of totality, indeed of the particular totality "desired and ordained by God."[4] The period from Jacob's sons to Salmon and Rahab encompasses not only seven generations, but also the period of history from the sojourn in Egypt and the exodus to the conquest of the land (Rahab), that is, the youth of the "son of God" Israel, who was "called out of Egypt."

The following two sections of the genealogy begin and end with interruptions of the genealogical schema. V. 6b mentions the woman by whom David was Solomon's father. The conclusion to this section gives an indication of time (v. 11a), which also opens the third section (v. 12a): "the deportation to Babylon." Furthermore, Jechoniah "and his brothers" are mentioned as sons, an anomaly v. 11a shares with v. 2c: Just as v. 2c marks the end of Israel's patriarchal period and the beginning of its national history by mentioning "brothers," so also does v. 11a mark the end of Israel's political history. Thus the period of the kings up to the exile is emphasized only at its beginning and end by an interruption of the schema, but exhibits no internal subdivisions. Is this coincidental? Or does it imply a theological judgment on the historical period of Judah's kings?

The post-exilic period is also not broken by any internal interruptions of the genealogical schema. The various generations serve only to continue life for the sake of the goal toward which the entire story moves. This goal, at the end of the third era, constitutes the most momentous interruption of the schema yet: Joseph is no longer mentioned as the procreator, but rather only as "Mary's husband." The procreator is concealed by the anonymity of the passive voice: "of whom Jesus was born, who is called Christ" (v. 16c, d). The subsequent commentary (v. 17) illuminates this mysterious passive: The Spirit of God

---

2. Idem, "Die Genealogie (Schlußteil)," *Biblische Zeitschrift* 9 (1965) 38.
3. Ibid., 36.
4. K. H. Rengstorf, *Theological Dictionary of the New Testament* II (1964) 628.

himself begets Jesus from the virgin Mary, the wife of Joseph. This shows that vv. 18-25 do belong with the genealogy.

The interruptions of the genealogical schema not only signal the text's division into subsections. Through similarities and contrasts they also indicate spatial relationships, so to speak, between textual components at levels transcending the succession of generations. Thus the titles given to David and Jesus (v. 6a; 16c, d) relate their names in the text, and the titles themselves are related, since "messiah" is the title of the eschatological "king" from the house of David. But this relationship alluded to by the structural similarity of "David the king" and "Jesus the Messiah" is nothing more than what the superscription (v. 1) has already expressed with the phrase "Son of David."

Furthermore, the few women mentioned in the genealogy may have in common that they all represent procreation in a foreign sphere: Tamar was actually Judah's daughter-in-law, the wife of someone else (Judah's eldest son Er). Rahab was a harlot, and thus the wife, so to speak, of many others. Ruth was a widow, and thus at least formerly the wife of someone else, and also a foreigner. Solomon was born after David's affair with "the wife of Uriah," a Hittite. "Mary" and "of the Holy Spirit" unite the two poles by having the least in common. But because of the women who have been mentioned, this is not completely without precedent.

The diagram on p. 138 represents the departures from a straightforward genealogical list brought about in this text by the metatextual material and the interruptions of the genealogical schema.

REDACTION CRITICISM AND TRADITION CRITICISM

The name "Emmanuel" is an established theme for Matthew. By giving Jesus this name, which means "God with us," at the beginning of the Gospel (1:23) and at the end in the words of the resurrected Jesus, "I am with you always, to the close of the age" (28:20), Matthew shows that his Gospel proclaims Jesus as the one in whom and through whom God is present with his people. This literary device of "inclusio," Matthew's framing of the entire Gospel, fuses the genealogy, which itself moves toward the "Emmanuel" designation, with the whole Gospel.

	I (vv. 2-6a)	II (vv. 6b-11)	III (vv. 13-16)
metanarrative statements:			
superscription (v. 1) "son of David"			Jesus
"son of Abraham"	Abraham ———————	David ———————	Jesus
commentary (v. 17): the number of generations	14	14 the exile	14
number of fathers in each group	13	14	13 ←
interruptions of the genealogical schema:			
titles		David the king ——————→	Jesus the Messiah
mothers	v. 2 | vv. 3-5a Tamar ——→ Rahab | vv. 5b-6a Ruth	the wife of Uriah	Mary
brothers	Judah's | Zerah		Jechoniah's
time indications		at the time of the deportation	after the deportation

Furthermore, the genealogy itself is construed with the Gospel in mind: Matthew emphasizes Jesus' sonship in Abraham because of the old promise that in Abraham "all the families of the earth will bless themselves" (Genesis 12:3). This promise is fulfilled, according to Matthew, through the "son of Abraham," Jesus: The resurrected Jesus instructs his disciples to "make disciples of all nations" (Matt 20:19), and it is to this end that he promises to be with them. Matthew picks up this theme immediately after the genealogy and the story of Jesus' birth through the Holy Spirit: Magi from the east come to Jerusalem as representatives of the Gentile nations blessed in this son of Abraham.

The Davidic sonship of Jesus is also a theme connecting the genealogy with the immediate context, that is, with the account of Jesus' infancy, and with the whole Gospel. The same is true of Jesus' divine sonship, to which the genealogy alludes in the irregularity of its schema and which it discloses by the story of Jesus' conception in the commentary in 1:17.

The Gospel and the genealogy are so interrelated that one must assume they were conceived as a unity at the very outset, and thus probably by the redactor of the Gospel of Matthew. Therefore, there is no real possibility of tradition criticism going behind the present text to a tradition that Matthew might have used, or of redaction criticism distinguishing this original version from its redactional reworking. Nor are there tensions in the text that might be used as points of departure for tradition-critical and redaction-critical work. We should conclude, then, that Matthew himself composed the genealogy and molded it with an eye on his own infancy story and his Gospel as a whole.

TRADITIONAL IDEAS

Procreation by the Spirit and Virgin Birth

This does not mean, however, that Matthew did not make use of certain established ideas, themes, and schemata passed down to him in tradition. One of these established traditions was that of Jesus' procreation by the Holy Spirit with the virgin Mary, Joseph's wife.

Although Luke and Matthew's infancy stories are independent of one another as far as sources are concerned, both are acquainted — and, we must add, they alone in the New Testament — with the idea of Jesus' procreation by the Spirit and his birth from a virgin. If one does not assume reminiscence in Jesus' family as the original setting of this idea, then one must view it as a theological expression of Jesus' ultimate origin from God, an expression that takes seriously, nonetheless, that he was born of a woman, that is, that he was human.

Comparison of Matthew and Luke shows that the background of the traditional idea was rendering of the "Immanuel" prophecy in Isaiah 7:14 in the Septuagint (the Greek translation of the Hebrew Scriptures), where Hebrew *'almâ* ("young woman") is represented by Greek *parthenos* ("virgin"). Some Christians took this passage as a prophetic reference to Jesus, and, indeed, the Septuagint's rendering of the passage had already paved the way for this interpretation.

For Isaiah the birth of a child was enough of a "sign" because God had indicated that it was to be such a sign. In later antiquity, however, in Jesus' own age, that is, only events that transcended the sphere of the ordinary — so-called "signs and wonders" — were taken as representing God's actions. This kind of thinking had to consider the alteration of the "young woman" of the Hebrew text into the "virgin" of the Greek text in a passage understood as a messianic prophecy as virtually providential. The story of a virgin conceiving and bearing a son without the participation of a man transcended the framework of the ordinary and prompted the suspicion that this son was a being that reached to the sphere of the deity himself, or indeed himself partook of the divine essence. This idea was all the more likely to catch on because of the belief, long held and widespread especially in Egypt, in any new king as procreated by a god with the royal earthly female.

To be sure, neither Matthew nor Luke materializes the idea to the point that Jesus' procreation by the Holy Spirit is taken as implying any bodily act. Such a notion was by no means alien to Gentiles, but a pious Jew was utterly incapable of such a crude understanding. But Jews did have some access to the idea of procreation through the Spirit by means of the concept of God's creative spirit.

That the New Testament attests the idea of the conception of Jesus through the Spirit only in Matthew and Luke shows that it was not a commonly held tradition in early Christianity. But it did later establish itself in the church at large and was accepted into the Apostles' Creed.

Son of David, Son of God

Another idea that Matthew incorporates into Jesus' genealogy is that of Jesus' identity as the son of David and the Son of God. Paul already attests this old traditional idea in Rom 1:3-4 in the context of a confession of faith passed down to him, probably by the church at Antioch. This confession probably read as follows:

> I believe in Jesus the Christ,
> born of David's seed according to the flesh,
> instituted the Son of God according to the Spirit of holiness,
> since the resurrection from the dead.

According to this confession, Jesus was the son of David already during his earthly existence ("according to the flesh"), but became God's Son only in his subsequent heavenly existence ("according to the Spirit of holiness") beginning with the resurrection from the dead, which commenced with him as the "first fruit of those who have fallen asleep" (1 Cor 15:20).

Although it may surprise us to hear of Jesus *becoming* God's Son, this idea becomes understandable against the tradition-historical background of the title "Son of God." In the ancient Near East and in Israel itself the king was considered from the moment of his enthronement to be the "son of God," that is, one whom the deity had adopted as son by means of an oracle. Psalm 2:7 gives us an example of this kind of adoption formula: The newly enthroned king proclaims:

> The Lord said to me:
> "You are my son,
> today I have begotten you."

The confessional formula cited in Rom 1:3-4 understands Jesus' exaltation by God as his enthronement as the eschatological king, that is, as his adoption and installation as the "Son of God." It also considers him in his earthly existence as the "son" from the "seed of David."

This idea of double sonship is related in tradition history to 2 Samuel 7. In the prophecy that Nathan is to give to David, God promises David to secure the throne for the son of David, that is, Solomon, and at Solomon's enthronement to accept him as his son, that is, as God's son: "I will be his father, and he will be my son" (2 Sam 7:14). But what initially serves only to secure Solomon's succession to the throne — which was disputed — by means of a "divine" oracle, is then expanded beyond Solomon to include the entire Davidic dynasty: "And your house and your kingdom will be made sure for ever before me. Your throne will be established for ever."

This oracle established itself and was incorporated into the sacred traditions of the kingdom of Judah. Even when after the exile no king from the Davidic line, no "son of David," took the throne again, Nathan's prophecy continued to be read and believed as sacred tradition and became the point of departure for anticipation of the Messiah. It came to be read, that is, as the promise that God would raise up a descendant from the house of David, a "son of David," would anoint him as the ultimate and final king of the end time, and would at his enthronement adopt him as God's son. The Jewish circles subscribing to this idea during Jesus' age anticipated the eschatological redeemer or Messiah as this one who is both "son of David" and "son of God," the eschatological king in God's service. Jesus did not apply these titles to himself, even if during his lifetime his appearance and deeds may well have awakened the expectation — and not just among his disciples — that he was indeed the son of David who would soon be installed as the messianic king.

Only after his death could Jesus be called "son of David" and "son of God" without causing misunderstanding, and only then could those titles be used to refer to his significance as the ultimate savior. Their meaning had been altered by his death on the cross. Now when one wanted to proclaim Jesus as the eschatological savior, one could assert that in his earthly life he was indeed this Davidic descendant, and that after his resurrection he was installed as the Son of God, as the heavenly messianic king and Lord. This is the substance of the confessional formula that Paul cites in Rom 1:3-4. During the course of tradition history, however, the point in time at which this messianic title was thought of as being bestowed on Jesus was moved back in time.

Mark already considers the earthly Jesus to be the enthroned messianic king. At the beginning of Jesus' public ministry, at his baptism, God bestows on Jesus the status of a king accepted as the Son of God: "You are my beloved Son. With you I am well pleased" (Mark 1:11 = Psalm 2:7 and Isaiah 42:1).

Matthew and Luke push the beginning of divine sonship even

further back. Already Jesus' procreation through the Holy Spirit makes him God's Son. This brings about a further alteration of the idea of the divine sonship of the messianic king, which originally had been based on adoption by God. His sonship is greater because of the combination of the idea of royal messianic divine sonship with that of spiritual procreation and virgin birth, which came from other sources.

For Matthew Jesus is, then, already the Son of God through his procreation, and Matthew is thus faced with the problem of the legitimacy of this "Son of God" as the "son of David." He solves this problem by using a genealogy, that is, a genre that functioned to secure a person's legitimacy by presenting an unbroken family tree. Therefore, Matthew's primary concern in the genealogy is not with establishing Jesus' divine sonship, but rather with his descent, at least legally, from David and Abraham.

This development reaches a provisional end in the New Testament with Paul and John. In their writings, the idea of a Son of God by divine adoption, originally at home in messianic thought, is combined with that of a "Son of God" existing even before creation itself. We have encountered this combination earlier, in our discussion of the tradition history of the New Testament hymns (chapter 12 above).

CHAPTER 14

The Beatitudes (and Woes)
(Matt 5:3-12; Luke 6:20-26)

Since the Beatitudes appear only in Matthew and Luke and not in Mark, we are probably correct in attributing them to the Q source.

Matt 5:1f. indicates a change of location to an "ideal setting" (that is, one created by the author, not a historical setting for the material that follows) and introduces Jesus' sermon with a solemn discourse introduction. The imagery that begins in v. 13 takes over after the Beatitudes. The Beatitudes themselves — vv. 3-12 — are thus the opening text of a larger textual whole; as such they are of decisive significance for the meaning of what is known as the "Sermon on the Mount" (chs. 5–7).

A similar situation is seen in Luke 6:17f. For the location the redactor chooses "a level place," hence the designation "Sermon on the Plain"; this enables a great multitude to hear the sermon. Yet the discourse introduction (v. 20) directs the discourse to the disciples. Here, too, the Beatitudes (and Woes) constitute the opening text of a larger discourse. This larger text in turn is both set off from and connected with the opening text in v. 27 by the address "to you" and the adversative conjunction "but."

THE FORM OF THE TEXT

The Structure of Matt 5:3-12

Matt 5:3-12 contains nine "macarisms" (from Greek *makarios*, "blessed") or "beatitudes." The basic syntactical structure (a nominal clause followed by a causal clause) occurs eight times in succession. Though the ninth beatitude (vv. 11-12) begins with the same word ("blessed"), it immediately departs from their form with a second person plural verb, while the eight preceding beatitudes are in the third person plural. The ninth beatitude is developed more extensively than the preceding eight, and its second person address is picked up in the immediately following context (vv. 13ff.).

While the first eight beatitudes are thus an interrelated block over against the ninth, they are still related to the ninth: Despite the differences, the ninth is still a beatitude, and by praising the "persecuted" it incorporates the theme with which the eighth beatitude concludes the block of the first eight.

The cohesion of the first eight beatitudes is strengthened by the use of inclusio, that is, by the catchphrase "kingdom of heaven" in the first and eighth. This might mean that these eight beatitudes have a consistent thematic focus, namely, the "kingdom of heaven" or the requirements for entry into the kingdom. This inclusio is strengthened by the use in the causal clauses of the first and eighth beatitudes of present tense "to be," while the second through seventh have causal clauses with future tense strong verbs referring to future rewards.

The verbs in the causal clauses of the second through fourth beatitudes are passive, active, and then passive, and this pattern is repeated in the fifth through seventh. These six beatitudes are thus arranged in two sections of three each. The break after the fourth beatitude is reinforced by the use of the catchword "righteousness" in the fourth and eighth beatitude, first as a desired goal and then as actualized righteousness for which one must suffer persecution.

So the entire series of eight is arranged into two sections of four each, and the intention of the overall testimony of this series of eight can already be summarized — in simplified form — as follows: "The kingdom of heaven is for the righteous, and will be allotted to them." The individual beatitudes explain who the righteous are and what the kingdom of heaven is.

Finally, the change from the third person plural of the first eight beatitudes to the second person plural address in the ninth corresponds to the emergence of the speaker in the ninth beatitude: "on my account." Therefore, the "righteousness" in view here is not abstract or objective, but arises only in reference to the speaker himself, that is, to Jesus.

The relationships among the nine beatitudes in Matthew are summarized in the diagram on p. 147.

The Structure of Luke 6:20-26

The main break in Luke 6:20-26 is signaled by the shift from beatitudes to woes after v. 23. The four beatitudes and the four woes are parallel in several respects:

- All the beatitudes and woes are in the second person plural of address.
- The first three beatitudes and the first three woes have the same basic syntactic structure, a nominal clause followed by causal clause.
- In the fourth beatitude and the fourth woe (vv. 22, 26) the normal syntactic structure is expanded.
- The causal clauses in the first beatitude and the first woe are in the present tense, so that both function as superscriptions for what follows.
- The causal clauses in the second and third beatitudes and the second and third woes are in the future tense.
- "Now" in the first clauses of the second and third beatitudes and the second and third woes amplifies the contrast between the present and the eschatological reversal.
- The beatitudes and woes correspond antithetically in content:

the poor	vs.	the rich
the hungry who are to be satisfied	vs.	the full who are to hunger
those weeping who are to laugh	vs.	laughers who will mourn and weep
the persecuted	vs.	those of whom all speak well.

- The first two beatitudes and the first two woes refer thus to physical distress or well-being, while the third and fourth beatitudes and woes address experiences that more immediately affect the spirit.

But this parallelism is not maintained throughout:

	vv. 1-2	v. 3	v. 4	v. 5	v. 6	v. 7	v. 8	v. 9	v. 10	vv. 11-12	vv. 13ff.
	setting and discourse introduction									expanded form, second person plural	second person address continues
		normal form, third person plural									
			strong verb, future tense						"to be," present tense		
verb in causal clause →			passive	active	passive	active	passive	passive			
"kingdom of heaven" →											
"righteousness" →											
persecution →											

147

- Second person plural "to you" occurs in the first clause of the first two woes, but not in the corresponding beatitudes or in the third woe; in the first woe it appears with a dative appositive ("the rich"), the only such appositive in the text.
- Only in the third woe does the causal clause use two verbs for the predicted future ("mourn and weep").
- The first clause in the fourth woe is shorter than the extended first clause of the fourth beatitude.
- Furthermore, the fourth woe does not have any elements answering to the fourth beatitude's imperative "Rejoice in that day, and leap for joy" or its reference to "reward in heaven."

The following diagram summarizes these similarities and differences:

beatitudes				woes			
second person plural							
v. 20	v. 21a	v. 21b	v. 22	v. 24	v. 25a	v. 25b	v. 26
normal form			amplified form	normal form			amplified form
physical distress		spiritual distress		physical well-being		spiritual well-being	
present	present and future			present	present and future		

SOURCE, TRADITION, AND REDACTION CRITICISM

If we assume (though not all scholars do) that Matthew and Luke are dependent in the Beatitudes on a common source (Q), then methodologically source and tradition criticism will work closely together, since the version antedating Matthew and Luke will be established less on the basis of tensions in the text than by comparison of the two extant versions. This also means that our investigation must simultaneously pose redaction-critical questions. The interdependence of the different exegetical methods is thus particularly evident here.

Source and Redaction

Both Matthew and Luke include the beatitudes of the poor, the hungry, the mourning/weeping, and the reviled. But the beatitudes of the mourning/weeping and the hungry are not in the same order in the two versions. Furthermore, Luke has nothing corresponding to Matthew's beatitudes of the meek, the merciful, the pure in heart, the peacemakers, and those persecuted for righteousness' sake, and Matthew has nothing corresponding to Luke's Woes.

Since we can find no reason for Matthew to omit the Woes if they were in his source, we may assume that they were created by the Lukan author as contrasts to the Beatitudes that he found in the source.[1] Similarly, we can find no reason to think that Luke deleted the beatitudes of the meek, merciful, pure in heart, peacemakers, and persecuted. They appear, rather, to have been Matthean creations, especially since they all praise those who actualize particular inner ethical attitudes and thus agree with the Matthean version of the four beatitudes that Matthew and Luke have in common. That is, Matthew does not praise merely the poor or the hungry, but rather the "poor *in spirit*" and "those who hunger *for righteousness*": External conditions become inner attitudes in the Matthean understanding of the beatitudes.

We are therefore probably right in believing that the Lukan beatitudes are closer to the original source in their number and wording than are Matthew's. Further evidence for this conclusion is found in use of favored Matthean terms, such as "kingdom of heaven" (vv. 3 and 10) and "righteousness" (vv. 6 and 10), and in the topical redundancy of the eighth and ninth Matthean beatitudes, which is characteristic of Matthean redaction.

But when we ask whether Q itself praised "those who *mourn*" (Matthew) or "those who ("you that") *weep*" (Luke), we notice that Luke has "mourn" in the corresponding woe. Much the same can be said of the phrase "they will be comforted" in the causal clause in Matt 5:4. Here, too, Luke follows the source in his construction of the woe (Luke 6:24), though he has not done so in the beatitude. The temporal specification "now" in the beatitudes of the hungry and the weeping is probably also a product of Lukan redaction: It strengthens the contrast between the present and the future and evokes the schema attested elsewhere in Luke of eschatological reversal of fortunes (cf. Luke 16:19-31, which contains material found only in Luke).

---

1. Cf. the woes or curses corresponding to beatitudes in Deuteronomy 28:3-6, 16-19; Tobit 13:12; *1 Enoch* 99:10ff.; 103:5; *2 Enoch* 52; *2 Baruch* 10:6-7.

In seeking to determine the original sequence of the beatitudes common to Matthew and Luke, we would have to give preference to Matthew's order, since the beatitudes of the poor and those who mourn recall the order in Isaiah 61:1ff. and because of the topical arrangement in the Lukan version, where physical distress ("poor" and "hungry") precedes distress of the spirit ("weeping" and "reviled"). This reordering of the second and third beatitudes of the source can be viewed as a Lukan redactional response to the blessing of those who are reviled, which itself already occupied the final position.

Matthew's use of the third person in eight of his nine beatitudes reflects the usual style of the genre of beatitudes.[2] The second person address in Luke's beatitudes corresponds, on the other hand, to the tendency in Christian tradition to address the believing community directly, which is also reflected in Matthew's ninth beatitude and in what follows it ("You are the salt of the earth," etc.).

Therefore, Matthew's use of the third person in his first three beatitudes is probably derived from his source. The beatitude of the reviled, on the other hand, where both Gospels use the second person, was probably in the second person in their common source. Thus the source already had an element of tension between the first three beatitudes and the fourth. (The Matthean and Lukan expansions in the fourth beatitude have increased this tension.) This tension prompts us to look even behind Q to the form the Beatitudes had before an apparent Q redaction. We will return to consideration of this earlier redaction after looking further at the beatitude of the reviled.

Matthean and Lukan Redaction of the Beatitude of the Reviled

Both Matthew and Luke set a series of clauses under a "when" in this beatitude (Matt 5:11; Luke 6:22; Luke has "when" twice), and both use the verb "revile" in one of these clauses. They also agree in giving a reason for the reviling (etc.) directed against those who are addressed.

2. Cf., e.g., Psalms 1:1; 2:12; 84:5; 128:1; Isaiah 30:18; John 20:29. Even where the person spoken *to* is the one spoken *of* in the beatitude, the beatitude can still be in the third person (Luke 1:45). The second person was used, though not to represent the readers/hearers directly (Deuteronomy 33:29; Ecclesiastes 10:17; Isaiah 32:20). See further K. Koch, *The Growth of the Biblical Tradition: The Form-Critical Method*, trans. S. M. Cupitt (New York: Scribner, 1969) 16-18.

That both Gospels use the word "evil" is a less significant common feature, since they use it in different ways.

Similarities in the explanatory sentences in Matt 5:12 and Luke 6:23 are limited to "rejoice" (though different Greek forms are represented by the identical translation), by the almost verbatim agreement in "for (behold) your reward is great in heaven" ("heaven" is plural in the Greek of Matthew), and in the reference to the prophets.

The differences in the two versions of this beatitude can be accounted for on the basis of redaction by one or the other of the Gospel writers. Examination of these differences thus leads us to a reconstruction of the beatitude as it appeared in Matthew and Luke's common source.

By adding the temporal designation "in that day" to the imperative "rejoice," Luke introduces the idea of eschatological judgment and thereby sharpens the contrast between the present condition of being reviled and future rejoicing over the heavenly reward. As in the beatitudes of the hungry and the weeping, where "now" is added in Luke, "in that day" thus introduces the Lukan schema of the eschatological reversal of fortunes. Luke also makes "people" (RSV "men") the subject of the abuse suffered by the blessed. This is not just a closer identification of Matthew's indefinite "they." Rather, by adding this subject Luke distinguishes the generation of those who mistreat the blessed from the generation of their "fathers" (which also appears only in Luke, in the last clause of v. 23), those who treated the Hebrew prophets in the same manner. He thus underscores his view of salvation history, in which the time of "the law and the prophets" is distinguished from the age of Jesus and the age of the church.

In Matthew — and the source — the continuity between the addressees and the "prophets" is accentuated more strongly by this use of this indefinite "they" for the abusers of both the blessed and the prophets. It is thus implied that the addressees are themselves prophets. If Matthew's "who were before you," which Luke does not have, is original, then even "the prophets" may have been, in Matthew and the source, not those of the Hebrew Bible (which they are in Luke's version, with "their fathers"), but Christian prophets who came before the addressees.

Though Matthew follows the source more faithfully than Luke does, he still puts his own redactional stamp on the treatment of the blessed and the prophets. He uses the catchword "persecute" of the fate of both — and has already introduced this theme in his redactional eighth beatitude. That the eighth and ninth beatitudes thus stand together in a mutually interpretative relationship is also evident from the use in both of "on account of" to identify the reason for the persecution. Matthew, who probably wrote during the reign of Domitian (ca. A.D. 85), most likely has in mind here early persecutions of Christians like those affecting his own church in Antioch.

Matthew also replaces the "Son of man" found in his source (Luke 6:22; as a concordance can show, Luke never introduces this christological title redactionally) with "on *my* account." For Matthew, "righteousness" is virtually identical with Jesus himself, who has come to perfect righteousness eschatologically in his teaching and to fulfill it eschatologically in his life (cf. Matt 1:15; 5:17).

"When people hate you" in Luke is almost identical to the remark by Tacitus (ca. A.D. 55-120) that Christians were "a class of people loathed for their vices" (*Annales* 15.44). It is, like Luke's specification of the subject as "people" rather than "they," probably redactional. If it were in the source, Matthew's failure to include it would be difficult to explain, since it would have fit well with his redactionally introduced situation of persecution. As the first of the abuses affecting the blessed, "hate" is that by which the other forms of abuse are interpreted in Luke: He is referring to ostracism of Christians by Gentiles.

But the motivation for this ostracism, "on account of the Son of man," shows that Luke did not come up with these formulations himself. "Son of man" is the language of tradition, not of Lukan redaction. In Luke's source "cast out your name as evil on account of the Son of man" probably refers to exclusion of Jewish Christians from the Jewish community because of their confession of Jesus as "Son of man" and Messiah. After the fall of Jerusalem to Rome in A.D. 70 Pharisaic leaders attempted to reestablish the identity of Judaism by excluding heterodox Jewish groups, among them Palestinian Jewish Christians. This situation is also implied by "when they exclude you," that is, in the situation of Luke's source, "when they excommunicate you from the synagogue." (A similar situation is reflected in John 9:22, where the parents of a man born blind are threatened with excommunication.) But with "when people hate you" Luke gives these expressions a different focus, looking instead to the situation of his Christian community in its Gentile environment.

For Matthew, too, the problem of excommunication of Jewish Christians by the Jewish community no longer plays any role. Although Judaism and Christianity still take notice of one another in Matthew, they have long since become separate entities. In the beatitude of the reviled Matthew deals with this change in a different way from Luke: He merely drops from his source those expressions ("exclude," "cast out your name") that are most explicitly linked to exclusion of Jewish Christians from the Jewish community.

We are now in a position to reconstruct the traditional text of the fourth beatitude as Matthew and Luke received it:

Blessed are you
when they exclude
and revile you
and cast out your name as evil
on account of the Son of man.

Rejoice
and leap for joy,
for your reward is great in heaven,
for so did they do to the prophets
[who were prophets] before you.

Source and Tradition Criticism of the Beatitude of the Reviled

Yet even this text exhibits tensions that allow us to develop further our source-critical hypothesis. According to the first part of the beatitude, the addressees are excluded (from the Jewish community) for confessing Jesus as the eschatological "Son of man." But the second part of the traditional beatitude likens the addressees to the "prophets" and thus reflects a situation in which they experience abuse because of some prophetic activity.

Matthew, as we have seen, apparently dropped "and cast out your name as evil on account of the Son of man" from the beatitude because synagogue excommunication was no longer a problem faced by his community. But in deleting this clause, he kept the word "evil," creating a new context for it: "and utter all kinds of evil against you falsely." He thus, as far as semantic intent is concerned, inadvertently came closer to a stage of tradition preceding his source.

At that earlier stage, the beatitude of the reviled did not yet contain any statements reflecting the situation of synagogue excommunication. But the beatitude was reworked after A.D. 70 in order to address just that situation. "When they exclude you" was added to the older source. "Cast out your name as evil," which was as peculiar in Greek as it is in English, resulted from the reformulation for that new situation of a clause that, despite its even stranger sound in English, meant, quite straightforwardly, "slander." That clause was "cast to you an evil name," and it fit quite well semantically with "when they revile you."

So the *original* form of the beatitude, prior to a redaction that resulted in the text as Matthew and Luke received it, spoke to those who were "reviled" in their Jewish environment and "slandered" "on account of the Son of man," that is, because they proclaimed the imminent parousia of Jesus, "the Son of man." The "prophets before you," that is, those who appeared earlier than the addressees, were figures such as John the Baptist or Jesus, not the prophets of the Hebrew Scriptures. John and Jesus prophesied the imminent coming of the Son of man as judge or of the kingdom of God. Their successors, those spoken to in the beatitude, were themselves prophetic preachers and prophetically proclaimed Jesus' imminent parousia as Son of man and judge. (It was Luke who first took the "prophets before you" to be those of the Hebrew Scriptures and who distinguished their era from that of the church.)

As we have seen, the first three original beatitudes were formulated in the declarative third person while the fourth was in second person direct address. This tension is resolved by the tradition-critical assumption that the beatitude of the reviled was added to the older beatitudes of the poor, the mourners, and the hungry, though at least as early as the Q redaction. Probably the "reviled" itinerant teachers of the earlier Q tradition composed this beatitude and applied it to themselves (addressed in the second person) as consolation in their situation of distress. They added it to the three original beatitudes, which Jesus had not intended merely as statements of consolation (hence his use of the third person). Later, before Matthew and Luke but after A.D. 70, this added beatitude was reworked in the Q redaction to apply to the exclusion of Jewish Christians from the Jewish community.

The Beatitudes as Spoken by Jesus

There is no reason not to attribute the first three beatitudes to Jesus. They fit well with what we are able to determine concerning his proclamation of the kingdom of God. It is even possible that they are part of Jesus' inaugural sermon commencing his public ministry and of the original form of his proclamation of the kingdom. In them he refers to Isaiah 61:1-2. His reading of those words of Isaiah disclosed to Jesus that he himself was sent to "bring good news to the poor" and to "comfort all who mourn."

Jesus used the third person as direct address in the Beatitudes because he was speaking of a specific group. In contrast, the declarative third person would address not a specific group, but everyone — including the rich, the glad, and the sated. The Beatitudes would be universal, timeless, and situationless principles. But the intention of the Beatitudes as spoken by Jesus was not consolation, but communication of principles valid only under the conditions of the inbreaking kingdom of God:

> The Beatitudes are misunderstood if we take them only as consolation to the poor, the hungry, and those who mourn. They are rather *proclamation of God's new order before the forum of the entire world,* and they address precisely those who are not poor, hungry, or in mourning. For them God is now proclaimed as the God of the poor, and his kingdom as the kingdom of the poor. God's kingdom — and this is asserted unequivocally — is genuinely his kingdom only when in it the poor receive justice. Here, then, Jesus destroys the false idea of "God for us" and "God with us," an idea that people construct according to their own desires and dreams. He also destroys the expectation that God's kingdom will accommodate itself to the interests of the individual and his or her group. He brings into the present the challenge directed against the legitimacy of the order that humankind has established according to the standards of power and gain.[3]

Summary: From Jesus to the Final Version

The hypothesis that we have arrived at can be briefly summarized and tested by a review of the stages of the text's development in chronological order:

Jesus' preaching, perhaps his inaugural proclamation of the kingdom of God, included the three beatitudes of the poor, the mourning,

---

3. P. Hoffmann, "'Selig sind die Armen. . . .' Auslegung der Bergpredigt II (Mt 5,13-16)," *Bibel und Leben* 10 (1969) 117.

and the hungry. He put them in the third person, as was usual for the beatitude form and as in Matthew, but without the Matthean additions "in spirit" and "and thirst for righteousness."

The early Q tradition, before A.D. 70, added to these three beatitudes a fourth, in the second person, directed to the reviled and slandered, that is, to the persecuted proclaimers of the imminent return of Jesus, the "Son of man." This fourth beatitude linked these itinerant Christian preachers to earlier suffering proclaimers of the Son of man, such as Jesus and John the Baptist, and applied Jesus' three beatitudes to the preachers, thus using what had been proclamation as consolation.

The later Q redaction altered this fourth beatitude to apply to the situation of synagogue excommunication after A.D. 70. It did so by adding "when they exclude you" and by altering the earlier tradition's "cast to you an evil name" (i.e., "slander you") to "cast out your name as evil." What was addressed to Christian preachers in the earlier Q tradition was thus applied more broadly to Palestinian Jewish Christian communities.

Matthew took over this Q redaction of the beatitudes, which spoke to a situation that no longer existed in his day, and altered it in several ways: He related the beatitudes more to inner attitudes by adding "in spirit" and "and thirst for righteousness" to two of the original three and by composing new beatitudes of "the meek," "the merciful," "the pure in heart," and "the peacemakers." He made them speak more clearly to a situation of persecution by adding a beatitude of those who are "persecuted for righteousness' sake" and by adding "persecute" to the beatitude of the reviled. He gave his themes of "righteousness" and "the kingdom of heaven" a strong place in this text and showed, with his references to righteousness, how being becomes action, how the righteousness of Jesus and the kingdom becomes the church's active righteousness. He clarified the link between the persecuted and Jesus by putting "on my account" in place of "on account of the Son of man." And he bound Jesus and righteousness together in the correspondence between "for righteousness' sake" and "on my account."

The Lukan redactor also reworked the Q redaction of the beatitudes: He recast the original three beatitudes in the second person. He added "now" to two of those three and "in that day" to the beatitude of the reviled to strengthen the contrast between present suffering and future rejoicing. He redirected the beatitude of the reviled to a situation of ostracism by Gentile society by adding "hate you." By adding "people" and "their fathers" to the beatitude of the reviled and by dropping "who were before you," he identified "the prophets" as those of the Hebrew Bible, thus forging a link of experience from those prophets to the people of his own Christian community. And he added a series of woes corresponding to each of his four beatitudes, thus strengthening their connection to his theme of eschatological reversal and making it evident that Jesus' statement that the kingdom belongs to the poor is a call to the conscience of Christians who are not poor.

CHAPTER 15

Form and Genre Criticism
of Paul's Letter to Philemon

Though letters have a relatively fixed form today, their form was even more strict in antiquity.[1] Paul was the master of New Testament letter writing. His letters synthesize genre elements from Hellenistic and Jewish letters into something completely new. He developed his own epistolary style, which characterizes all his letters and had great influence on the rest of New Testament epistolary literature.[2]

Paul's short letter to Philemon is well suited for illustrating the style of Paul's letters. When we describe the individual form of this letter we are engaged in *form criticism,* as we have defined it in chapter 4. When we compare this form with those of Paul's other letters, we are engaged in *genre criticism.*

THE EPISTOLARY MACROSTRUCTURE

Paul's letter to Philemon follows the normal tripartite structure of epistolary genre:

---

1. For an introductory survey see S. K. Stowers, *Letter Writing in Greco-Roman Antiquity* (Philadelphia: Westminster, 1986), or, more briefly, D. E. Aune, *The New Testament in Its Literary Environment* (Philadelphia: Westminster, 1987) 158-82.
2. For a survey see W. G. Doty, *Letters in Primitive Christianity* (Philadelphia: Fortress, 1973) 21-47.

- Letter opening (proemium)
- Letter body
- Letter closing

Among these general structures, the letter body exhibits the least inclination toward fixed form and the least use of the particular genre features that enable us to compare one letter with others. The body is, instead, where the situation prompting a letter and the specific content of the letter's response to that situation exert the most influence.[3] Therefore, a specific discussion of the letter body of Philemon is not needed for our purposes here.

In contrast, the epistolary opening and closing follow fixed patterns more closely. Paul put together his own version of these patterns within the patterns of ancient letter writing in general. Our discussion of the typical elements found at the beginning and end of Philemon will be guided by this outline:

- Letter opening (vv. 1-9)
  - prescript (vv. 1-3)
    - sender (v. 1a-b)
    - addressee (vv. 1c-2)
    - salutation (v. 3)
  - thanksgiving (vv. 4-7)
  - self-commendation (vv. 8-9)
- Letter body (vv. 10-20)
- Letter closing (vv. 21-25)
  - concluding parenesis (vv. 21-22)
  - greetings from others (vv. 23-24)
  - benediction (v. 25)

THE LETTER OPENING

Prescript

The prescript has two parts corresponding to (1) a modern letter's letterhead and inside address and (2) a modern letter's greeting ("Dear . . .").

---

3. On the letter body see further J. L. White, *The Form and Function of the Body of the Greek Letter* (Missoula: Scholars, 1972).

The first of these two parts of the prescript indicates the letter's senders in the nominative case (the *superscriptio:* "Paul . . . and Timothy . . .") and its recipients in the dative case (the *adscriptio:* "to Philemon, . . . Apphia, . . . Archippus, . . . and the church in your house"). Both the senders' and the addressees' names are accompanied by titles or honorific epithets (*intitulationes:* "a prisoner for Christ Jesus," "our brother"; "our beloved fellow worker," "our sister," and "our fellow soldier").

In the second part of the prescript, the salutation, Paul builds his own form on the basis of the corresponding elements of Greek and Jewish letters. In Greek letters the salutation was "rejoice" *(chaire),* but Paul uses the related word "grace" *(charis).* In Jewish letters the salutation was "peace" (Hebrew *šālôm* = Greek *eirēnē*). Paul also emphatically Christianizes these elements of the salutation by indicating the origin of the "grace and peace" he wishes for the addressees: "from God our Father and the Lord Jesus Christ" (v. 3).[4]

Despite this fixed schema, the unique character of each letter of Paul can be discerned already in the prescript. All of his letters are addressed to churches, except, it appears, this letter "to Philemon," which at first glance looks like a personal letter. But Philemon, to whom the letter is directed ("you" is singular in vv. 4-24), is only one of the co-addressees, who include two other individuals and an entire house church. What at first appears to be a personal letter turns out to be a letter to a church.

That the epistolary prescript includes individuals as addressees is a departure from the other Pauline letters, and this is prompted by the letter's circumstances. Philemon is addressed in regard to his slave Onesimus, who has escaped and will in the normal course of events be branded a fugitive — literally with the letter *F* on his forehead. But already in the address of the letter Paul makes it clear that this is not a purely private matter between himself and Philemon. As far as the treatment of his slave and Christian brother Onesimus is concerned, Philemon is to act as a member of a Christian community. And by

---

4. Today scholars tend to attribute to Paul a more creative role in the composition of his letters, and downplay the assertion that he combined stylistic elements of Greek and Jewish letters. It is clear that "grace" and "peace" acquire in Paul's letters a specific meaning related to Pauline christology, to his doctrine of justification, and to the various circumstances prompting his letters.

placing Philemon before the forum of the believing community in the prescript of the letter, Paul also ensures that Philemon can no longer deal with Onesimus privately, since the matter is now known to others.

Paul's variation of the fixed schema of the epistolary prescript thus already enters into the circumstances prompting the letter. Though the prescript is part of the epistolary macrostructure, it is not simply an unalterable formulaic feature. It bears important topical material and as such is closely related to the rest of the letter.

Thanksgiving

In most of Paul's letters the prescript is followed by Paul's statement that he always thanks God for the addressees (in this case, a singular addressee) when he (or: and that he) remembers the addressee(s) in his prayers (v. 4). Here, too, Paul follows the custom of other ancient letters, which often include a "remembrance" motif, that is, a section in which the writer describes how vividly he remembers the recipient. This motif evokes — for the writer — the person of the recipient as a partner in the dialogue for which the letter is a substitute. The wording of the remembrance motif can, then, call forth for the recipient a sense of being honored or flattered. Where such a motif occurs in spoken discourse as a deferential gesture on the part of the speaker toward the audience, we call it *captatio benevolentiae*.

The more a letter goes beyond friendly small talk and conversational niceties in its pursuit of a specific goal — as is the case here in Paul's concern for the treatment of Onesimus — then the more it is a substitute for discourse and the more the epistolary remembrance motif will itself be consciously goal-oriented. It will in such a case focus on specific characteristics of the addressee that serve the rhetorical goal that the letter, as a substitute for actual dialogue, pursues.

Paul embeds the remembrance motif in thanksgiving to God. Here he reflects Hellenistic Jewish expressions of thanks and praise (note the eulogy in place of thanksgiving in 2 Cor 1:3ff.). Gentile letters "remember" characteristics of their recipients, but Jewish letters praise or thank God when evoking their recipient's good traits.

But as with the prescript, Paul also Christianizes this part of the letter. He does so by making one God-given character trait the basis for all the other traits mentioned, namely, faith in Christ (v. 5). He knows that what he describes of the recipient ultimately comes from God. God has given Paul himself this fundamental gift of faith, and this faith is, then, the framework for the specific characteristic of the recipient that he thanks God for. In the letter to Philemon the specific characteristic is Philemon's "love for all the saints." This love — and this is the goal that the letter body will seek to actualize — should manifest itself further in Philemon's benign treatment of Onesimus.

Paul's epistolary thanksgivings normally end with what is called the "eschatological climax,"[5] in which he expresses his confidence or wish that the addressees, whose God-given faith the thanksgiving recalls, might preserve that faith and attain its goal, which is eschatological salvation. Here again Paul follows already existing epistolary style. Ancient letters often employed the *formula valetudinis*, the writer's wish for the addressee's health and well-being,[6] and this wish could be expressed in religious terms. For Paul, the ultimate "well-being" that he wishes for his addressees is the fulfillment of their eschatological participation in salvation, itself based on the faith that God has given them, which must nonetheless persevere until this fulfillment.

But there is no such eschatological climax in the letter to Philemon. Once Paul has mentioned Philemon's faith in Christ and love for fellow Christians, it is sufficient to wish for continued manifestation of these traits in "the knowledge of all the good that is ours in Christ," that is, in the matter that the letter addresses. If Philemon is generous in his treatment of Onesimus, who has become a brother in Christ, then his "love for all the saints" has, indeed, been manifested in this knowledge.

Self-Commendation

We have already seen that the epistolary thanksgiving can be understood in terms of spoken discourse as a *captatio benevolentiae* through which the speaker seeks to gain the sympathy of his hearers. The focus in the *captatio* is on the audience, or, in an epistolary thanksgiving, on the

5. P. Schubert, *Form and Function of the Pauline Thanksgivings* (Berlin: Töpelmann, 1939), *passim*.

6. E.g., "The old Romans had a custom which survived even into my lifetime. They would add to the opening words of a letter: 'If you are well, it is well; I also am well.'" So Seneca, *Epistulae Morales*, trans. R. M. Gummere (Loeb Classical Library; New York: Heinemann, 1937) II, 95 (letter 15, to Lucillus).

addressee. An oral speech would move from the *captatio* to a section in which the speaker draws the hearers' attention to himself and seeks to prove his competence and authority before beginning the main part of his discourse. A letter, too, might have a section before the letter body in which the focus shifts from the recipient to the writer and his epistolary authority and competence.

The epistolary self-commendation in the letter to Philemon (vv. 8-9) exhibits the close relationship of this section to spoken discourse. It does so in the rhetorical device of coupling renunciation of any claim to authority with mention of the authority and in the device of appeal to the addressee's sympathetic emotions. It is in keeping with the character of this epistolary section that the writer comes out fully in the light of his self-portrayal. Furthermore, use of the writer's name reminds the recipient of his personal ties to the writer.

The self-commendation occurs in all the Pauline letters immediately before the letter body. It is developed differently in each letter, but its function remains the same. It is most fully developed in 1 Cor 1:10–4:21, where it comes to be a fundamental discussion of the essence of the Pauline apostolate.

THE LETTER CLOSING

In the letter body (vv. 10-20) the specific dominates and stylistic features characterizing the epistolary genre recede. But in the letter's conclusion (vv. 21-25) the genre asserts itself again with the concluding parenesis, postscript, which consists of greetings from others and a concluding benediction.

Concluding Parenesis

The concluding exhortation or parenesis is well developed in most of Paul's letters. But due to the brevity of the letter to Philemon, it encompasses here only two verses (vv. 21-22). It is, nonetheless, identifiable as the concluding parenesis by its use of typical elements and in that it carries out the typical function of such a section, which is to present the practical consequences of the "teaching" in the letter body, that is, to complement the letter's indicatives with imperatives. In the parenesis in this letter Paul again urges Philemon — though only obliquely — to treat Onesimus in the way that the letter body suggests: "knowing that you will do even more than I say."

Paul includes another element typical of the concluding parenesis of New Testament letters when he announces to Philemon that he will be coming for a visit. This reference to his own plans is a form of what has been called the epistolary "parousia."[7] One of the prerequisites of a letter is distance between writer and recipient. Such distance threatens an established friendship, and, according to ancient epistolary theoreticians, one of the bases of friendship is proximity; one defeated this threat with letters, which are substitutes for personal dialogue. Thus one could compensate for physical absence by spiritual presence.

Because Paul attributed great significance to his personal presence in his relationships with churches, he made much use of the Hellenistic epistolary "parousia."[8] In the epistolary thanksgiving at the beginning of a letter he might recall his presence at the founding of the addressees' faith community. He might also announce a coming visit in the concluding parenesis. Here, since Paul has just announced such a visit, Philemon will be all the more motivated to follow Paul's request made in the letter.

Postscript

Greetings

The letter to Philemon does not include an element found in the concluding sections of other Pauline letters, namely, instructions to the recipients to pass on greetings, which was sometimes in the form of a directive to "greet one another with a holy kiss" (e.g., 1 Thess 5:26). Earlier interpreters believed that the "holy kiss" was evidence that Paul's letters had a liturgical setting. The kiss marked, so it was thought, the

---

7. *Parousia,* a Greek word meaning "presence," is normally used in theological contexts of Christ's expected return. Here, however, it is used of an epistolary motif referring to forms of the writer's "presence" with the recipient.

8. See R. W. Funk, "The Apostolic Presence: Paul," in *idem, Parables and Presence: Forms of the New Testament Tradition* (Philadelphia: Fortress, 1982), 81-102.

transition from the reading of the letter before the congregation to the liturgy.[9] More recent studies have shown that the significance of the kiss directive is epistolary and is determined by each letter's specific circumstances.[10] Friends normally greeted one another with an embrace and a kiss, and the Christian "holy kiss" was nothing more than a form of this normal greeting. Paul's directive to "greet one another," perhaps "with a holy kiss," was intended to encourage the individual who had received the letter to inform as many members of the church as possible that the letter had arrived.

This makes it understandable that the conclusion to the letter to Philemon dispenses with the injunction to deliver greetings: Already in the prescript the letter addresses itself not only to Philemon himself, but includes the forum of the entire congregation, presumably to keep the letter from being understood as purely personal.

But Paul's conveyance of greetings from others is particularly developed in this letter (vv. 23-24), and for a similar reason. Paul delivers greetings from five fellow workers, all mentioned by name. He thus tells the letter's recipient that the matter discussed in the letter is also known to the Christians with Paul. Now Philemon cannot easily ignore the letter. Here as elsewhere we must interpret Paul's directive to deliver greetings (or, in this case, the lack of such a directive) and his conveyance of greetings from others from the perspective of each letter's particular circumstances.

Benediction

In ancient letters the final element (the *eschatocol*) was the greeting of the letter writer. Paul follows this form, but with obvious differences. Another ancient letter closes with "Fare well, even if you must do so as a scoundrel. May the gods protect you." Paul's form of greeting is a benediction: "The grace of the Lord Jesus Christ be with your spirit." Letters were often actually written by scribes (e.g., Tertius in Rom 16:22), but at the end of a letter, the author, who had been dictating to that point, would take the pen from the hand of the scribe and write the

9. So G. Bornkamm, "On the Understanding of Worship," in idem, *Early Christian Experience,* trans. P. L. Hammer (New York: Harper and Row, 1969) 161-79.

10. K. Thraede, "Ursprünge und Formen des 'Heiligen Kusses' im Frühen Christentum," *Jahrbuch für Antike und Christentum* 11/12 (1968) 124-80.

concluding greeting with his own hand as a sign of the letter's authenticity. The handwritten greeting thus fulfilled approximately the function that a signature does in a modern typed or printed letter.

Signatures fulfilled a different function in antiquity. They were used particularly in legal contexts and thus served to validate documents. In the letter to Philemon (v. 19) Paul's signature validates a declaration of compensation.

Paul's signature also has legal implications in 1 Cor 16:21; Col 4:18; 2 Thess 3:17. In 1 Cor 16:21 a post-Pauline writer uses Paul's signature, not to imply that the letter comes from Paul, which is already clear, but to give certain elements in the letter — both Pauline and post-apostolic elements (the latter including the prohibition of women teaching) — the status of binding apostolic regulations valid for the whole church. Similarly, the authors of Colossians and 2 Thessalonians use Paul's signature to give their pseudonymous letters not so much an appearance of authenticity as a quasi-legal status.

CHAPTER 16

Books to Aid the
New Testament Exegete

This final chapter provides a list of books that describe and exemplify the different steps in and approaches to New Testament exegesis or that provide other important resources for the New Testament exegete. The best use of these works will be what is implied by the title above: Though some of them could be used as substitutes for independent exegesis, all of them can and should be, instead, aids to your own exegetical work. This list is by necessity selective. It provides only a beginning in each of the areas that it covers.

BOOKS ON NEW TESTAMENT EXEGESIS

A primary aim of the book before you has been to give the growing number of theological students who have not studied Greek — and may never do so — access to the methods of responsible exegesis. The emphasis has been on exegetical methods that focus on levels of language that are not bound to any one language and therefore permit those without knowledge of Greek to engage in meaningful and valid exegetical work. We have also emphasized procedures that transcend the parameters of individual sentences and focus more than traditional exegesis on what gives each text its distinctive identity. There are other books on New Testament exegesis, but these have been the special aims of this one.

But because other voices can be helpful, our bibliography begins with some other introductions to exegesis, some focusing on the New Testament and some treating the whole Bible:

H. Conzelmann and A. Lindemann, *Interpreting the New Testament: An Introduction to the Principles and Methods of New Testament Exegesis* (Peabody, MA: Hendrickson, 1988)
G. D. Fee, *New Testament Exegesis: A Handbook for Students and Pastors* (Philadelphia: Westminster, 1983)
O. Kaiser and W. G. Kümmel, *Exegetical Method: A Student's Handbook* (New York: Seabury, [2]1981)
G. Lohfink, *The Bible: Now I Get It! A Form Criticism Handbook* (Garden City, NY: Doubleday, 1979)
D. Lührmann, *An Itinerary for New Testament Study* (Philadelphia: TPI, 1989)

Somewhat different are multi-author works that examine each aspect of New Testament criticism in turn and that are a bit more theoretically oriented than the present book and the books listed above:

D. A. Black and D. S. Dockery, *New Testament Criticism and Interpretation* (Grand Rapids: Zondervan, 1991)
I. Howard Marshall, ed., *New Testament Interpretation: Essays on Principles and Methods* (Grand Rapids: Eerdmans, 1977)

Another book of the same kind, but with greater emphasis on literary approaches to the text, is forthcoming in 1994 from Eerdmans under the editorship of Joel Green. Serving similar purposes are two dictionary-format reference works:

R. N. Soulen, *Handbook of Biblical Criticism* (Atlanta: John Knox, [2]1981)
R. J. Coggins and J. L. Houlden, *A Dictionary of Biblical Interpretation* (Philadelphia: TPI, 1990)

The books listed so far deal mainly with exegetical methods and procedures, not with underlying hermeneutical issues. For brief introductions to such issues, see the articles on "Hermeneutics" by W. G. Jeanrond in the *Dictionary of Biblical Interpretation* (listed above), 282-84, and by B. C. Lategan in the *Anchor Bible Dictionary* (listed below), III, 149-54.

Understanding of the methods of critical exegesis is reinforced by knowledge of how those methods have developed. Such knowledge of the history of New Testament exegesis can be gained from these two books:

W. G. Kümmel, *The New Testament: The History of the Investigation of Its Problems* (Nashville: Abingdon, 1972)
S. Neill and T. Wright, *The Interpretation of the NT 1861-1986* (New York: Oxford, 1988)

A good orientation to *current* approaches and understandings of New Testament scholarship is offered by:

E. J. Epp and G. W. MacRae, ed., *The New Testament and Its Modern Interpreters* (Philadelphia: Fortress, 1989)

BIBLE DICTIONARIES

Bible dictionaries and encyclopedias (no difference is implied by the use of one or the other of the two terms) can come into use at nearly every stage of exegesis. They provide help with regard to every topic mentioned in this bibliography and are often the best place to turn first.

As you continue to work at biblical exegesis, you will find your needs for information going beyond what is normally provided in one-volume Bible dictionaries. All the dictionaries listed here are large, multi-volume works in which nearly every article is written by a scholar particularly able to report on the subject of the article. The *Interpreter's Dictionary* is a classic and very useful compendium of moderate scholarship. The *International Standard Bible Encyclopedia* is equally comprehensive and represents more conservative scholarship. The *Anchor* dictionary is the most up-to-date of those listed and has several articles of particular help in regard to fundamental issues of exegesis. Hastings's *Dictionary* is older than the others, but generally treats historical questions in greater detail.

G. W. Bromiley, et al., ed., *The International Standard Bible Encyclopedia* (four volumes; revised edition; Grand Rapids: Eerdmans, 1979-88)

G. A. Buttrick, et al., ed., *The Interpreter's Dictionary of the Bible: An Illustrated Encyclopedia* (four volumes; Nashville: Abingdon, 1962; supplementary volume, ed. K. Crim, et al., 1976)

D. N. Freedman, et al., ed., *The Anchor Bible Dictionary* (six volumes; New York: Doubleday, 1992)

J. Hastings, et al., ed., *A Dictionary of the Bible* (four volumes; New York: Scribner, 1898-1902; supplementary volume, 1904)

Literary Genres of the New Testament

An essential aspect of exegesis is identification of the genre of the text one is faced with and of characteristics of the text that are conditioned by its genre. The following book deals with each of the main literary types represented in the New Testament in relation to writings of the same or similar genres from the time of the New Testament:

D. E. Aune, *The New Testament in Its Literary Environment* (Philadelphia: Westminster, 1987)

Another book examines the literary types of the New Testament books and the subgenres contained in them:

J. L. Bailey and L. D. Vander Broek, *Literary Forms in the New Testament: A Handbook* (Louisville: Westminster/John Knox, 1992)

Each of the main literary types represented in the New Testament calls for its own variations of the fundamental exegetical methods. So we deal with each in turn.

Historiography

The main point of contact in the New Testament with ancient historiography is the book of Acts, though issues with regard to historiography and historicity obviously come into play in regard to the Gospels as well. The following work examines the book of Acts in the light of ancient historiography:

M. Hengel, *Acts and the History of Earliest Christianity* (Philadelphia: Fortress, 1979)

The New Testament's historiographical context is examined for itself in:

C. W. Fornara, *The Nature of History in Ancient Greece and Rome* (Berkeley: University of California, 1983)

The Gospels

A synopsis of the Gospels is always needed when one is working with a passage from the Synoptic Gospels. The standard synopses in English are:

K. Aland, ed., *Synopsis of the Four Gospels* (New York: American Bible Society, [9]1987)
B. H. Throckmorton, ed., *Gospel Parallels: A Synopsis of the First Three Gospels* (Nashville: Nelson, [3]1967)

The New Testament exegete should be acquainted with the classic works on Gospel form criticism by Bultmann and Dibelius:

Rudolf Bultmann, *History of the Synoptic Tradition* (New York: Harper and Row, [2]1968)
Martin Dibelius, *From Tradition to Gospel* (New York: Scribner, 1965)

Bultmann also wrote a briefer presentation of his work in Gospel form criticism:

"The Study of the Synoptic Gospels," in *Form Criticism: Two Essays on New Testament Research,* by R. Bultmann and K. Kundsin (reprint, New York: Harper and Row, 1962)

Subsequent scholarship has criticized classical Gospel form criticism in a number of ways. See, for example:

E. Güttgemanns, *Candid Questions Concerning Gospel Form Criticism* (Pittsburgh: Pickwick, 1979)

A brief treatment of the history and practice of Gospel form criticism is found in:

E. V. McKnight, *What is Form Criticism?* (Philadelphia: Fortress, 1969)

A useful survey of the history of interpretation of the Gospels and of continuing issues, focusing mainly on the "historical Jesus" question, is found in:

W. B. Tatum, *In Quest of Jesus: A Guidebook* (Atlanta: John Knox, 1982)

It is worthwhile to be acquainted with this classic work in Gospel redaction criticism:

G. Bornkamm, G. Barth, and H. J. Held, *Tradition and Interpretation in Matthew* (Philadelphia: Westminster, 1963)

Much of the ancient literature that has similarities in genre to parts of the Gospels is translated in:

D. R. Cartlidge and D. L Dungan, *Documents for the Study of the Gospels* (New York: Collins, 1980)

Finally, a study of the gospel genre as it is found not just in the canonical Gospels but also in Q and in noncanonical gospel literature is offered in:

H. Koester, *Ancient Christian Gospels: Their History and Development* (Philadelphia: TPI, 1990)

Letters

Two introductory works on ancient letter genres with an eye toward the New Testament letters are:

W. G. Doty, *Letters in Primitive Christianity* (Philadelphia: Fortress, 1973)
S. K. Stowers, *Letter Writing in Greco-Roman Antiquity* (Philadelphia: Westminster, 1986)

A classic work in epistolary form criticism is:

P. Schubert, *Form and Function of the Pauline Thanksgivings* (Berlin: Töpelmann, 1939)

Finally, we list a useful aid in study of the structural and thematic similarities of Paul's letters that is similar to the Gospel synopses mentioned above:

F. O. Francis and J. P. Sampley, *Pauline Parallels* (Philadelphia: Fortress, ²1984)

Apocalyptic Literature

The New Testament book of Revelation has been a focal point in the development of understanding of the apocalypse genre. Mark 13 and its parallels in Matthew and Luke are also apocalypses, and it may be argued that apocalyptic thinking provides much of the framework of the message of Jesus and the rest of the New Testament. Introductory discussions of the apocalypse genre are found in these works by J. J. Collins:

J. J. Collins, *Daniel, with an Introduction to Apocalyptic Literature* (vol. XX in The Forms of the Old Testament Literature; Grand Rapids: Eerdmans, 1984) 1-24

J. J. Collins, *The Apocalyptic Imagination: An Introduction to the Jewish Matrix of Christianity* (New York: Crossroad, 1984) 1-32

Also quite helpful is the article on "Apocalypses and Apocalypticism" by A. Yarbro Collins, J. J. Collins, A. K. Grayson, and P. D. Hanson in the *Anchor Bible Dictionary* (see above) I, 279-92. A helpful collection of essays on apocalyptic literature is found in:

P. D. Hanson, *Visionaries and Their Apocalypses* (Philadelphia: Fortress, 1983)

THE WORDS OF THE NEW TESTAMENT

It is of course in study of the language of the New Testament that the shortcomings of working in English rather than Greek are most obvious. But a number of works provide information on the language of the New Testament in forms accessible to the student who has not (or has not yet) studied Greek. Intelligent use of a concordance is especially fundamental to the exegetical task. Concordances of the Greek text include:

W. F. Moulton, A. S. Geden, and H. K. Moulton, *A Concordance to the Greek Testament* (Edinburgh: Clark, [5]1978)

Concordance to the Novum Testamentum Graece of Nestle-Aland, 26th Edition, and to the Greek New Testament, 3rd Edition (Berlin and New York: de Gruyter, [3]1987)

Analytical concordances allow one to work back from an English translation to the Greek text with little or no knowledge of Greek. The only complete analytical concordance of a modern English version of the Bible is:

R. E. Whitaker, *The Eerdmans Analytical Concordance to the Revised Standard Version of the Bible* (Grand Rapids: Eerdmans, 1988)

Works in dictionary format on the history and usage of New Testament words require varying amounts of knowledge of Greek, from none (Brown's three volumes) to at least the alphabet (the ten volumes of Kittel and Friedrich and the three volumes of Balz and Schneider, both made accessible by English indexes) and to what would be gained in a single-semester course in New Testament Greek (Bauer, et al.):

H. Balz and G. Schneider, *Exegetical Dictionary of the New Testament* (Grand Rapids: Eerdmans, 1990-93)

W. Bauer, W. F. Arndt, F. W. Gingrich, and F. Danker, *A Greek-English Lexicon of the New Testament and Other Early Christian Literature* (Chicago: University of Chicago, [2]1979)

C. Brown, ed. *The New International Dictionary of New Testament Theology* (Grand Rapids: Zondervan, 1967-78)

174

G. Kittel and G. Friedrich, *Theological Dictionary of the New Testament* (Grand Rapids: Eerdmans, 1964-76)

The lexicon prepared by Nida and Louw is also made accessible by an English index. It is different from the works listed above in that it focuses on semantic relationships among words rather than on the history of usage of words:

J. P. Louw and E. A. Nida, *Greek-English Lexicon of the New Testament Based on Semantic Domains* (New York: United Bible Societies, 1988)

New Testament scholarship has been affected in a number of ways by developments in linguistics, and the Nida-Louw lexicon reflects much of that influence. An older work applying linguistic study to the New Testament, one that contains still relevant warnings regarding our treatment of New Testament language, is:

J. Barr, *The Semantics of Biblical Language* (Oxford: Oxford University Press, 1961)

Two other useful works applying linguistic study to biblical exegesis are:

G. B. Caird, *The Language and Imagery of the Bible* (Philadelphia: Westminster, 1980)
P. Cotterell and M. Turner, *Linguistics and Biblical Interpretation* (Downers Grove, IL: InterVarsity, 1989)

THE NEW TESTAMENT'S HISTORY AND HISTORICAL SETTING

In biblical studies "introduction" is most often used as a technical term for the study of issues involved in the historical origins of the different biblical books, that is, their authorship, date, geographical provenance, and the like. Three of the most useful comprehensive works of New Testament introduction are listed below. Lohse's is by far the briefest of the three.

B. S. Childs, *The New Testament as Canon: An Introduction* (Philadelphia: Fortress, 1984)

W. G. Kümmel, *Introduction to the New Testament* (Nashville: Abingdon, [2]1975)

E.. Lohse, *The Formation of the New Testament* (Nashville: Abingdon, 1981)

Comprehensive reconstructions of the history of the church during the period in which the New Testament documents were written include the following books, Conzelmann's the briefest and Bruce's representing more conservative positions on many matters:

F. F. Bruce, *New Testament History* (Garden City, NY: Doubleday, 1969)

H. Conzelmann, *History of Primitive Christianity* (Nashville: Abingdon, 1973)

H. Koester, *History and Literature of Early Christianity* (= *Introduction to the New Testament*, vol. 2; New York: De Gruyter, 1982)

Information regarding the geographical contexts of the New Testament documents can be gained from atlases of the Bible. Among the many published, one that is particularly convenient and inexpensive is:

H. G. May, ed., *Oxford Bible Atlas* (London: Oxford, [3]1984)

Useful overviews of the historical and cultural background of the New Testament are provided in:

H. Koester, *History, Culture, and Religion of the Hellenistic Age* (= *Introduction to the New Testament*, vol. 1; New York: De Gruyter, 1982)

E. Lohse, *The New Testament Environment* (Nashville: Abingdon, 1976)

B. Reicke, *The New Testament Era: The World of the Bible from 500 B.C. to A.D. 100* (Philadelphia: Fortress, 1964)

J. E. Stambaugh, *The New Testament in Its Social Environment* (Philadelphia: Westminster, 1986)

Many of the historical source documents of the time of the New Testament and a good sampling of the literature of the time are available in:

C. K. Barrett, ed., *The New Testament Background: Selected Documents* (San Francisco: Harper and Row, ²1987)

Much of what the interpreter needs to understand about the New Testament's historical setting can be placed under the heading of the interaction between Judaism and Greco-Roman culture and politics. A classic work on that interaction is:

M. Hengel, *Judaism and Hellenism: Studies in their Encounter in Palestine during the Early Hellenistic Period* (Philadelphia: Fortress, 1974)

Also quite useful is a briefer work from the same author:

M. Hengel, *Jews, Greeks, and Barbarians: Aspects of the Hellenization of Judaism in the Pre-Christian Period* (Philadelphia: Fortress, 1980)

A detailed picture of Judaism and the Jews at the time of the New Testament is provided by the essays in the two volumes of:

S. Safrai and M. Stern, ed., *The Jewish People in the First Century: Historical Geography, Political History, Social, Cultural, and Religious Life and Institutions* (Philadelphia: Fortress, 1974, 1976)

Equally comprehensive and with a greater focus on history and literature is the revision of Schürer's history in three volumes (bound as four):

E. Schürer, *The History of the Jewish People in the Age of Jesus Christ,* ed. G. Vermes, F. Millar, and M. Goodman (Edinburgh: Clark, 1973-87)

The following two works are on Gentile religions of the time of the New Testament, the first a selection of translated source documents, the second a discussion, accessible to the beginning student, of Gentile religions as the background of the early development of Christian understandings of God:

F. C. Grant, ed., *Hellenistic Religions: The Age of Syncretism* (Indianapolis: Bobbs-Merrill, 1953)
R. M. Grant, *Gods and the One God* (Philadelphia: Westminster, 1986)

The Results of New Testament Exegesis

This book has intentionally avoided referring to many secondary works in its discussions of particular New Testament passages. By mastering the methods of New Testament exegesis, you will increasingly be able to engage in responsible biblical scholarship with a certain degree of independence. Turning too quickly to scholarly works of exegesis can inhibit this growth of exegetical skill. At the least, it is more effective to work through the steps of exegesis independently before turning to the results of exegesis done by others. In this way, those other interpreters, though they may be scholars with years more experience, can be conversation partners in understanding the New Testament, rather than unquestioned masters.

Commentaries on books of the New Testament are obviously a fundamental form in which the results of exegesis are presented. The continuing publication of numerous new commentary series and independent commentaries is testimony not only to their popularity among Bible readers, students, and preachers, but also to their simple usefulness as presentations of exegesis. Anyone who has worked through the present book should consult only commentaries meant to supply just that: scholarly exegesis. Lack of knowledge of Greek becomes a difficulty in regard to only a minority of points in commentaries on the Greek text. Even for preaching it is best to apply the exegetical methods to the text independently and then to be in conversation with exegetical scholars.

Current commentary series that consistently represent the results of scholarly exegesis include The International Critical Commentary (published by T. and T. Clark), Hermeneia — A Critical and Historical Commentary on the Bible (published by Fortress Press), the Anchor Bible (published by Doubleday), the Word Biblical Commentary (published by Word Books of Waco, TX), and The New International Greek Testament Commentary (published by Eerdmans). Series in which some volumes present scholarly exegesis are The New International Commentary on the New Testament and The New Century Bible Commentary (both from Eerdmans) and Harper's (= Black's) New Testament Commentaries (most recently reprinted by Hendrickson).

Many important exegetical commentaries are independent volumes. That is, they are not published as volumes in commentary series (though some began life in German series). These include R. Gundry on Mark (Eerdmans), R. Bultmann on John (Westminster),

E. Haenchen on Acts (Westminster), E. Käsemann on Romans (Eerdmans), Bultmann on 2 Corinthians (from Augsburg Press of Minneapolis), J.-F. Collange on Philippians (from Epworth Press in London), and L. Goppelt on 1 Peter (Eerdmans).

"Biblical theology" is in a sense the end product of biblical scholarship. Works of biblical theology (which usually treat only the Hebrew Bible/Old Testament or the New Testament, but not both) synthesize the results of broad biblical study (though the degree of synthesis varies greatly among the different works). The interface of biblical studies with the other theological disciplines is most obvious in biblical theology. Recent works in German (by P. Stuhlmacher, H. Hübner, and others) show that New Testament scholarship has clearly not done away with the synthesizing approach of biblical theology. Among the works listed here, Bultmann's is a classic that must always be consulted, Conzelmann's is a briefer work indebted in many ways to Bultmann, Goppelt's represents to some extent a conservative (though not predictably conservative) response to Bultmann and his students, and Ladd's represents North American conservative evangelicalism.

R. Bultmann, *Theology of the New Testament* (New York: Scribner, 1951, 1955)

H. Conzelmann, *An Outline of the Theology of the New Testament* (New York: Harper and Row, 1969)

L. Goppelt, *Theology of the New Testament* (Grand Rapids: Eerdmans, 1981, 1982)

G. E. Ladd, *A Theology of the New Testament* (Grand Rapids: Eerdmans, [2]1993)

Behind the broad presentations of exegesis in commentaries and New Testament theologies stand scholarly articles and monographs that often deal in greater detail with matters of exegesis. The most important scholarly journals that include articles on New Testament topics all or most in English are *Novum Testamentum, New Testament Studies, Journal for the Study of the New Testament, Catholic Biblical Quarterly, Interpretation, Journal of Biblical Literature,* and *Biblical Interpretation.* Journal articles, essays in special volumes, and monographs on particular New Testament topics can be located with the aid of *New Testament Abstracts, Religion Index One: Periodicals, Religion Index Two: Multi-Author Works, Elenchus Bibliographicus Biblicus,* and *Internationale Zeit-*

schriftenschau für Bibelwissenschaft und Grenzgebiete, which are periodicals devoted entirely to bibliography. Furthermore, nearly every book
listed above has some sort of bibliography, sometimes lengthy and comprehensive.

Index of Scripture References

Pages set in boldface include detailed discussion of the references.